What is
Global History?

For Albert and Odile

What is
Global History?

PAMELA KYLE CROSSLEY

polity

First published in 2008 by Polity Press
Reprinted in 2008 (twice), 2014, 2015, 2017, 2018

Polity Press
65 Bridge Street
Cambridge CB2 1UR, UK.

Polity Press
350 Main Street
Malden, MA 02148, USA

ISBN-13: 978-07456-3300-8
ISBN-13: 978-07456-3301-5 (pb)

A catalogue record for this book is available from the British Library.

Typeset in 10.5 on 12 pt Sabon
by SNP Best-set Typesetter Ltd., Hong Kong
Printed and bound by CPI Group (UK) Ltd, Croydon, CR0 4YY

The publisher has used its best endeavours to ensure that the URLs for external websites referred to in this book are correct and active at the time of going to press. However, the publisher has no responsibility for the websites and can make no guarantee that a site will remain live or that the content is or will remain appropriate.

Every effort has been made to trace all copyright holders, but if any have been inadvertently overlooked the publishers will be pleased to include any necessary credits in any subsequent reprint or edition.

For further information on Polity, visit our website: www.politybooks.com

Contents

Acknowledgments

This book was originally suggested to me by Polity, and I appreciate the suggestion. All my colleagues and co-authors in world and global history have influenced me in ways too numerous and subtle to understand, let alone acknowledge, though I am sure they will show through in the text. I have greatly benefited from the kind reading of early drafts and suggestions for further reading from several colleagues at Dartmouth, of whom Steven J. Ericson and Ronald Edsforth were particularly generous.

I wish to thank the editors at Polity Press, particularly Andrea Drugan, for their great patience. The readers provided indispensable corrections, challenges, and sufficient encouragement. Jennifer Speake's sharp eyes have much improved the text. I appreciate Polity's indulgence in resolving some punctuation subtleties in favor of the author's American training.

Introduction

H. G. Wells, best known today as the writer of science fiction classics such as *The Time Machine* and *The War of the Worlds*, also wrote one of the most influential global histories, *Outline of History*, first published in 1920. In the introduction Wells confronted the fact that few of his readers had any idea of what a "universal" history was. He lamented that too many people avoided studying history at all. Should they learn the long and complex history of England, then they knew only the history of England. Surely, to be really educated in history, they would also need to learn the history of France, and Germany, and Russia, not to mention other nations very far removed from Wells's own place and time. But to learn enough history to have a full grasp of human experience was a task too large for any single individual. Wells advised,

> the only possible answer is that universal history is at once something more and something less than the aggregate of the national histories to which we are accustomed, that it must be approached in a different spirit and dealt with in a different manner. This book seeks to justify that answer. It has been written primarily to show that *history as one whole* is amenable to a more broad and comprehensive handling than is the history of special nations and periods, a broad handling that will bring it within the normal limitations of time and

energy set to the reading and education of an ordinary citizen.[1]

Wells was not the first to state this idea, or indeed to attempt a "universal" history, but the idea was not well received anyway. In the great universities of Britain and the United States, departments of history – which in many cases were less than a decade old as of 1900 – taught only the history of the classical Greek and Roman world, European history, and (in the United States) American history. Other histories were taught in what we would now call "regional studies" departments. An "oriental" studies department would teach Chinese language, philosophy, and history. A "Slavic" studies department would teach Russian language, literature, and history, and so on. Historians often simply did not believe that studying regions outside Europe and North America would teach anything about the lessons of change over time. When the great transformative passages in history – revolution, nationalism, industrialization, secularization – occurred in regions outside Europe or North America, they were regarded as mere imitations or echoes of what had already happened in Europe.

Many historians, if asked, might have said that this was a matter of the division of labor. People have to study a great deal of their own national history, but only a minimal amount of foreign history. The justification for such an idea could certainly be debated, but whatever the usefulness of dividing "national" and "foreign" histories, historians as professionals have changed so much that they would probably all agree that is impossible to understand the great changes in human history without considering the whole earth. Not only is it a possibility that future changes originating in Asia, Africa, or Latin America will change the world, it is a fact of the past.

Historians in Wells's own time were attempting to broaden historical study by simply adding more national histories, in just the way that he ridiculed. A history department today would not imagine that they could achieve competence in "world," "global," or "universal" history merely by adding

1 Wells, *Outline of History*, 4th edn (1921), p. v.

more and more historians, each doing the history of a nation or region. A sufficient number of historians could never be added, and a curriculum that would allow students to absorb the available histories could never be devised. On the contrary, global history requires a method that is quite different from what is normally used to teach a narrative national or regional history. It is by their methods, more than their facts, that global historians are distinguished from those doing regional or national history. These methods sometimes cause friction among historians, but as we will see the result is a symbiotic relationship. Global historians supply what regional historians cannot, and the opposite is also true.

We might return to Wells's *Outline of History* to begin to see how this relationship works. Wells's idea was that paleontologists, archeologists, anthropologists, and historians as groups (and sometimes generations of these professional groups) could produce information that would reveal patterns, and that the universal historian would use the study of those patterns to explain the dynamics that cause change – in the past, the present, and the future. The specifics of Wells's ideas regarding these universal patterns will be discussed later, and they would be regarded as controversial today. But his basic understanding of universal history as the work done not by primary researchers, but by those who review that research to seek patterns of general relevance, still defines what we understand today as "universal," "global," or "world" history. There are no documents, artefacts, or personal testimony that allow us to research global history. The essential work of discovering facts and assembling primary history is not the work of those doing global history. Rather, they draw on the research done by other historians, making comparisons, noting large patterns, and proposing ways of understanding change that will clarify the nature and the meaning of all human history.

Sometimes the distinctions between these tasks – between primary research on the one hand and the review of primary research for purposes of finding patterns of causation – is delineated in scholarly fields as the difference between those who are practitioners and those who are "philosophers." In physics, for instance, there are the scientists who are in the laboratory testing hypotheses or investigating new phenomena, and there are those who are in libraries or studies reviewing the research in order to understand the meaning of the knowledge being gained. The historian Edward Gibbon thought that the greatest histories would be written by "historian-philosophers," who would review all known research and come to understand not only cause and effect in history, but the ways in which the past is perceived by historians and others.[2] As we will see, global or universal historians are not the long-sought philosophers of history who can resolve the great questions. Though they necessarily work from historical scholarship and not from original historical documents or artefacts, they have more in common with other social scientists than with philosophers.

As Wells noted, terms such as "universal," "comprehensive," "world," or "global" (or, today, "macro") history not only suggest that the scope of information is unlimited, but also imply the necessity to impose a single structural or causal explanation upon an infinite variety of human perspectives and experience. As will become apparent, some writers of great or comprehensive histories have indeed attempted these impossible tasks. But others have focused on understanding a limited number of phenomena that not only apply to diverse experiences – and perhaps to all experience – but also offer the possibility of explaining change over time in many different circumstances. Such historians have attempted to limit their arguments to specific topics that both they and their readers can understand. In the most successful of these projects, historians have been able to accommodate both the unlimited diversity of human culture and perspective, and the basic unifying institutions that let us know we are all one species, experiencing one history, on one earth.

The conundrum that global history has set itself is how to tell a story without a center. It is not certain this can be done. The ultimate global history device, should it be realized, would not be text, or story arc, or an analytical concept. It would more likely be a context spinner, that at one moment can sequence events and statistics from the perspective of a material or device (such as Shelagh Vainker's study of silk,

2   Evans, "Notes," from Gibbon, "Essai sur l'étude de la litterature"; see Carr, *What is History?*, p. lvii.

or Mark Kurlansky's on salt, or Staller and colleagues' on maize, or Barbara Freese's on coal, or Finkelstein and McCleery's on the book), or a behavioral concept (such as Michel Foucault on sexuality, or William McNeill on dance and drill) or a natural phenomenon (such as de Boer and Sanders's study of the historical impact of earthquakes). To spin sequentially a perspective of history centered on Ethiopia, or the pentatonic musical scale, or KIT chromosomal rearrangements, or interest rates would be desirable; to spin them simultaneously would be excellent; to have patterns extract themselves objectively from infinite simultaneous perspectives would be ideal. Unfortunately, language and narrative stay within the limits of grammar, vocabulary, and a unidirectional sense of time, and the moment of matching form and content has not yet arrived. Global historians are always working in suspense.

Though we often think of "world" or "global" history as recent subjects for study – Wells, after all, knew that his audience in 1920 understood historical study as ancient, but "universal" history as recently fashionable – the fact is that the earliest histories were always told with an assumption that they accounted for all people in one way or another. In fact, most cultures regard history as a story – indeed in European languages the meanings of the word "history" have followed a trajectory from factual inquiry to story-spinning that parallels the development of historical practice itself – and the impulse to tell stories on grand or universal scales is fundamental in most cultures. As we will see, many great religious traditions and most cultures preserve an original story about the beginnings of the universe or the creation of mankind. Some of these stories are still regarded as historical at least in part, and even those now relegated to the category of "myth" remind us that from early times people tended to narrate human experience as a great whole, and not as merely the adventures of local tribes, clans, or nations. This tendency to be inclusive for purposes of understanding the deep factors behind change and development is, perhaps, universal. Though it does not in method resemble much of what global or world historians do today, it accounts in part for the continuing fascination with the ideal of a universal history. It is something that cannot be distilled from the modern mission of global explanation, and it is discussed in this book as one of the sources of the modern global historical intellectual heritage.

As new methods of researching and writing history emerged in the medieval, the early modern and the modern periods, methods of thinking about the reasons for change, and its effects on human society, changed too. When centralized nation-states became dominant over much of the world in the sixteenth and seventeenth centuries, histories began to focus on the national groups – often defined by language, homeland, or sometimes religion – as the primary historical actors. The fashion for richly detailed stories of the emergence of specific peoples – sometimes from the wilderness, sometimes from under imperial domination – was reinforced by the actual phenomenon of national emergence and state-building in the nineteenth and early twentieth centuries. Indeed, well into the twentieth century the structure of all historical narrative was dominated by the archetypical story of each nation's cultural evolution and political emancipation, sometimes followed by its ability to expand and dominate other peoples. For the century between about 1850 and 1950, all history was, to one degree or another, national history or a compendium of geographically related national histories. This was the trend that Wells feared would overwhelm the ability of any individual reader to see history as significant. He hoped to restore the meaning of history for the individual reader by creating a new literature of the large lessons and theories of causation that could be derived from the wealth of detailed historical knowledge that the universities and libraries of his time contained.

In the aftermath of World War I, European historians and other writers blamed nationalist passions for the tragedy, and looked with greater interest to the theories of the social scientists who had not only regarded nationalist narratives as trivial and vain, but seemed to have predicted the outbreak of the "Great War." History, like all other fields of thought, was greatly affected by the cultural ferment of the 1920s and 1930s, as the global economy collapsed and competition among nations became sharper. Socialists, pacifists, imperialists, anarchists, and fascists all entered the fray, attempting to find an explanation for history that would solve the puzzle of how the world had got into crisis and how it could get out. But the decades of skeptical treatment of nationalism by historians with a universal or comparative outlook could not suppress the still-rising tide of nationalism and nationalist histories. Much of Asia and Africa, and Latin America, was emerging from a period of domination by European imperial powers. They, too, sought illumination and national justification from history. Kinds of historical thought inherited in one way or another from Karl Marx and his materialist contemporaries were adapted to both nationalist and universalist purposes by historians all over the world. Even Marx's most direct intellectual descendants sought to adapt his unforgiving materialist and universalist scheme to more local, subjective, and indeed nationalist purposes. Ideas about history were intertwined with every ideological struggle, whether nationalist or universalist, that marked the world so deeply as it approached World War II.

Following that conflict, it seemed that entrenched and defensive ideologies created seemingly unbridgeable schisms between historians living under communist governments and those living in self-described capitalist countries. In the Soviet Union, the People's Republic of China, and many countries of Asia, Africa, and Latin America where communism was encouraged or tolerated by the government, historians insisted that the great global struggle, both in the past and in the present, had been between countries encouraging the concentration of wealth and using imperialism to expropriate the wealth of less militarily powerful people on the one hand, and nationalist leaders attempting to fight off imperialism and improve their people's well-being on the other. In North America, Western Europe, and other countries in the world allied with them, historians insisted that greater relative wealth and power were the products of superior cultures, or healthier social systems, or political cultures in which governments permitted freedom of thought and speech. They saw human history as being a struggle between states and societies seeking totalitarian domination, on the one hand, and the people seeking freedom of thought and action, including the right to pursue their own material advancement, on the other.

In the mid-twentieth century, history as a discipline was influenced very markedly by new disciplines of the social sciences. In the late nineteenth century, sociology – like anthropology, economics, and political science – had been developed from studies of history. Using these new and overtly "scientific" disciplines, scholars looked to the past to discover the fundamental causes of change around the world, not merely in the individual countries that historians had been concentrating on for decades. Anthropologists such as William Dean Howells, Mary Douglas, Marcel Mauss, Claude Lévi-Strauss, Eric R. Wolf, Jack Goody, and Colin Renfrew; philosophers such as Michel Foucault; sociologists such as Barrington Moore, Immanuel Wallerstein, Charles Tilly, Michael Mann, and Christopher Chase-Dunn; political scientists such as Karl Wittfogel, Perry Anderson, Theda Skocpol, and David Wilkinson; and biologists such as Jared Diamond have all been among the practitioners of these allied disciplines who have influenced the emergence of the large-scale historical interpretations that we now call "world" or "global" histories. Historians from Arnold Toynbee and Oswald Spengler in the early twentieth century to Fernand Braudel at mid-century to William McNeill and his students today, established the modern style of large-scale historical analysis.

Understanding the variety of approaches used by historians and other scholars writing global history can be as complex as attempting to understand the history itself. Analytical concepts and philosophical approaches have been borrowed from the social sciences into global history, sometimes refined and given back again. Most approaches to global history carry within them the seeds of their own critique, and sometimes their own negation; as a consequence, a great deal of writing by global historians is about method and concept. Some of what appears or is announced to be new is actually old. Some of what is claimed to be universal is actually parochial. Some of what is promoted as objective is actually subjective. As historians assess themselves and others, approaches to global history can change rapidly. In fact, the idea of "universal" or "global" history encompasses a true variety of genres. As we will see, a bundled set of assumptions and perceived problems lies behind the dominant and well-developed "world" history genre. "Global" history is still an emerging enterprise, with a sharply different set of assumptions and questions. Related to all, but neglected in this book for want of space, are comparative historians, cultural historians, and international historians; though their work is related to global history, they have distinct concerns and methods.

In order to introduce the basic theories and methods that have defined global history, and to arrange them in some very rough chronological order, I have lumped them under very general categories. The categories themselves are meant to suggest both analytical concepts and narrative strategies, which for all historians – and global historians perhaps above all – are inseparable problems. First is "Divergence," or the narrative of things diversifying over time and space from a single origin. Next is "Convergence," or the narrative of different and widely spaced things necessarily assuming similarities over time. Then comes "Contagion," or the narrative of things crossing boundaries and dramatically changing their dynamics at the same time. Last is "Systems," or the narrative of interacting structures changing each other at the same time. My colleagues might well disagree with me not only about whether the categories are useful but also about exactly which writers and which works belong in which category, and how many subcategories there might be. Indeed, I might have changed them all had I written the book a year later. Nevertheless, this structure has seemed to me to be the most heuristically valuable at this time. Most readers will, I hope, see that these are not only categories of analytical thinking but also maps for narrative construction. Treatment of the categories is preceded by a discussion of the meaning and persistence of the great story impulse in our cultures. A conclusion links the categorical discussions with the problems of narrative and the assumed meanings of history to assess where global history is now and where it might go.

In addition to the organization, the book uses a few conventions that, again, are chosen for their heuristic and narrative value more than for their ability to render intellectual satisfaction. One is an implied chronology of Eurasian orientation. There is a "classical" time, a "medieval," an "early modern," and a "modern" period. These are not, to my mind, exclusively European in reference; they can be linked to widespread developments in Eurasian history generally. That does not make them genuinely "world" and far less "global" concepts; it only makes them useful for guiding writers and readers toward a language of world or global chronologies. They are familiar to most readers and are probably harmless so long as the reader knows enough to accept them in the heuristic spirit in which they are offered. The same is true for other terms that are employed despite a lack of precision or strict correctness. Examples include, but are not limited to, Byzantine empire, Zimbabwe, India, China, South America, sub-Saharan Africa, and Germany.

By design, this book is an introduction, and like all works of its kind must omit ninety-nine items out of hundred. The writers discussed are selected transitional figures in some cases, in others exemplars. I regret that very many interesting and important scholars have been omitted, and warn the reader against understanding this book as anything more than a brief introduction to the issues and techniques that make global history distinctive. Many specific subjects – including almost all technologies, including cartography – have been sacrificed to analytical themes and problems. A bibliography is provided to allow readers to follow their interests to more sophisticated levels, and to learn of the work of the many excellent writers who have put their shoulder to the wheel of universal history.

Suggestions for further reading

Dunn, Ross E., *The New World History: A Teacher's Companion.* Boston MA: Bedford/St Martin's, 1999.

Hodgson, Marshall G. S., *Rethinking World History.* Cambridge: Cambridge University Press, 1993.

Manning, Patrick, *Navigating World History: Historians Create a Global Past.* New York: Palgrave Macmillan, 2003.

Mazlish, Bruce, *The New Global History.* London: Routledge, 2006.

Wells, Herbert George, *The Outline of History: Being a Plain History of Life and Mankind.* New York: The Macmillan Company, 1920.

1
The Great Story Impulse

Before the age of writing peoples told stories, and usually began at the point that humanity came into existence. When they related the differentiation of their own group, they necessarily included the history of the rest of humanity by contrast or by comparison. In this way, people transmitting myths about their own origins inevitably told a general history of the world. Once writing became established, the major religious traditions all taught great stories of the creation of the world and the common experience and questions of all early people. As with the origin myths of people with oral traditions, the religious narratives also told the story of all people by attempting to tell the story of only one. For every people that migrated, others did not, or migrated somewhere else. For each people entering into a compact with a particular deity, or with a supreme god, others did not. For each people attacked or enslaved, somebody else was the attacker or the enslaver.

From earliest times, groups of people defined themselves as groups by telling their histories. In many cases they traced themselves back to founding animal spirits that assumed human form, had the power to have human offspring, or could transfer their qualities to humans through contact. The Romans, for instance, thought that part of their special character and destiny derived from the fact that the orphan boys Romulus and Remus were raised by a motherly wolf. Koreans told a story of a bear transformed through its own hard work into a human who became the father of the first Korean king. The Mongols considered themselves the descendants of a wolf father and doe mother. In other cases, the people narrated themselves as the intentional creation of supernatural entities. The Mayan creation myth tells of gods experimenting with making humans out of mud and wood before being counseled by primeval animals on how to make perfect humans. The early Japanese told a story of the simultaneous creation of their islands and people by the parents of the sun goddess Amaterasu, while the ancient Hebrews told of the first man (and in some versions the first woman) being fashioned from clay by God.

The story preserved in the Hebrew Bible is perhaps the best-known and most elaborate ancient history of the peopling of the earth. From the first humans grew a population that became strongly differentiated in its means of living, its places of residence, and its loyalties to local leaders. This early diversity was destroyed in a great flood, which reduced humanity to another very small group, clearly differentiated into three branches who ultimately separated from each other to pursue their own cultures. Many other cultures also tell myths of a catastrophic flood that reduced humanity to a small and struggling group. Archeologists, geologists, mythologists, and biologists are still attempting to solve this riddle of shared narratives. It is certainly possible that as the last Ice Age dissolved about 10,000 years ago water levels rose in many parts of the world, perhaps devastating many settlements and isolating the survivors. As recently as 5000 years ago, it is possible that a global trauma occurred that sharply affected temperatures and sea levels. It is also possible that separate water disasters – early floodings of the Yellow River in China, inundations of the shores of the Black Sea in western Eurasia, the eruption of the volcano of which a fragment is now called Santorini in about 1500 BCE, or tsunamis after volcanic eruptions in the Pacific, for instance – are remembered in stories that are superficially similar but originated in very separate events.

The Hebrew Bible is noteworthy for its detailed treatment of peoples in addition to the Hebrews. Local peoples with distinct cultures, languages, and religions, the Sumerian and

Babylonian empires, and the Egyptian pharaohs, their courts, and officials all figure in the history. But among ancient texts the Bible is not unique in this regard. Other early works inform us of the vivid awareness of many ancient peoples that they did not inhabit a world alone, and that in the world there was diversity of culture and philosophy. The Vedas of early India, for instance, frequently mention the enemy peoples, their gods, their customs, and even their technologies. But perhaps the closest narratives to compare to the Hebrew Bible in terms of international detail and interest are the oral histories woven into epic form by the author or authors known to us as "Homer." In them, peoples of the Greek mainland and islands struggle with foreign peoples of Asia Minor (Anatolia) and various regions of the Mediterranean.

Coming within about three hundred years of the Vedas – roughly the seventh to the fifth centuries BCE – the *Gilgamesh* epic of ancient Iraq, the *Iliad* and *Odyssey* attributed to Homer, and the *Mahâbhârata* and *Râmâyana* of ancient India all joined the Hebrew Bible among long and politically important early written stories. It is not surprising that in all these epics travel, migration, conquest. and personal battles figure prominently; this was an age of population rise, urbanization, and competition for good farmland, grazing land, and harbors. Long-distance sea trade in the Mediterranean, West Africa, and the Persian Gulf reached unprecedented volume.

The ancient Chinese classics, describing the period of roughly 3500 years ago, mention not only their own ancestors but also other peoples who were not agricultural, who were apparently nomadic, who spoke their own languages, lived in their own regions, and worshipped their own gods. The story of China's early "Three Sage Emperors" is partly the story of the conquest or the driving away of these neighboring cultures. As in the Hebrew Bible, genealogies, religious ideas, technologies, and localities are brought together to present a picture of distinct peoples, aware of their distinctness, competing to establish their own security or dominance.

Ancient peoples who left strong narrative legacies generally displayed distinct traits. They tended to have rich agricultural and commercial aspects to their economies, which brought them into regular contacts with other peoples and usually provoked certain competition for land and resources. In connection with this, they tended to experience sufficient population growth to support military elites, significant armies, and organized expansion into lands normally inhabited or dominated by distinct neighbors. They usually had priestly or scholarly classes, who had the time and specialized training to memorize, lecture on, and sometimes research stories about the past. And they almost always had writing systems that they used to preserve their histories and disseminate them to other places and times.

Greeks of the sixth and fifth centuries BCE were among the earliest writers to make story-telling into history, and we tend to focus on Herodotus (484–425) as a transitional figure. The Greek world was one of relatively advanced geographical knowledge, and it had an industrious class of scholars and teachers who not only committed to writing the oral traditions of Greeks and related peoples but also studied the contemporary writings of travelers and diplomats to work out an understanding of the larger world. In his own time Herodotus was not regarded by his colleagues as completely reliable or original, but modern scholars attribute some special achievements to him. Most striking, perhaps, was his use of the word "history" (in his own writing a Greek word meaning "to investigate," or "to come to know") to describe the use of documents, testimony, and, when possible, artefacts to test the stories that came from the past and present. Herodotus was explicit in saying that the stories must not be accepted at face value, but subjected to verification whenever possible. Of ancient Greek writers whose work survives, Herodotus gives us the earliest and clearest prescription for a more objective approach to understanding the past.

Though no saga creator in the style of Homer, Herodotus still thought of space and time in the sense of the travels, challenges, and triumphs of individual humans. The Persian rulers, the enemies of the leaders of Greek civilization, were depicted as credible human beings, and while Herodotus' characterization of Persian civilization was not flattering, he nevertheless clearly appreciated it as a coherent, complex society with structure and values. Herodotus' use of the word *oikoumene* (ecumene) was intriguingly ambiguous. Whereas many other writers seemed to use it to refer to the world of Greek hegemony, Herodotus seems to use it to mean the known world of human settlement. In this respect he may be the predecessor of later authors using the word to mean universal, global, or the "world." Herodotus is also one of our main channels for understanding the strong and continuing connections of the Mediterranean cultures with East, North and West Africa. Indeed his famous passage, based on the voyages of Hanno of Carthage (modern Tunis) around the coast of Northwest Africa, noted that though Hanno's captains thought they traveled west, the sun was on their right. In this way, narrative becomes geography, as Herodotus suggests that the true outline of the African continent could be deduced from such details in explorers' accounts. Though insisting that the practice of inquiry was different from the writing of oral tales, Herodotus nevertheless also was adamant that in the final analysis meaning is rendered in the large-scale, confirmed story as related in vivid writing.

With the emergence of empires controlling vast terrains and establishing the foundations of classical civilizations during, roughly, the fourth century BCE to the fourth century CE, history-telling became something based even more extensively on writing, and individual historians were able to preserve their own researches and narratives in fixed form. In all these cases, the perspectives of the historians were very much those of the empires they served. They saw the birth and expansion of their empires as lifting up the material well-being and cultural accomplishments of the world. They looked out upon neighboring peoples, particularly those who were military enemies, as strange and barbaric. They mostly approved of the cultural expansion of their empires – the imposition upon neighboring peoples of the imperial people's ways of writing, observing the laws, organizing families, and doing business – as bringing greater uniformity, rationality, efficiency, and justice to the world. Whether the Greek Herodotus, or the Chinese Sima Qian (145–90 BCE), these historians carefully narrated their sagas of the expansion of their empires over the fragmented, illiterate, putatively barbaric, and unenlightened peoples around them.

Very rich history and comment emerged from many of these empires between about 100 BCE and 500 CE. This was the age in which the Silk Roads were established across Eurasia, and in which some cultures incorporated knowledge of sails and trade winds to undertake long-distance ocean travel for the first time. Most of these early compilations took the form of geographical treatises. Many were based on the accounts of soldiers and merchants who had traveled to the edges of their empires and beyond. On occasion, they also incorporated second-hand information that the writers had gathered in their travels about places they had never been. Greeks wrote in detail, if not always with sympathy, of Macedonia, Persia, Egypt, parts of the Middle East, and northwest India. Romans wrote histories of the Germans, the Celts, and the Huns. The Chinese wrote of the peoples of Southeast Asia, of northern and northwest India, of western Iran, of Central Asia, of Siberia and Northeast Asia, of the Koreans, and eventually of the Japanese. On the basis of knowledge gained in the ancient kingdom of Sindh (roughly, modern Pakistan), the Greeks were able to learn of the Chinese, and the Chinese of the Greeks, before they had substantial contact in person. Megasthenes, a Greek traveler, was in the region about 300 BCE and wrote an extensive report. The Chinese traveler and military commander Zhang Qian travelled as far as the Bactrian and Parthian provinces of Iran between 136 and 126 BCE. Only a few years later, the historian Sima Qian was able to write of Sindh that their culture resembled the culture of western Iran, that they had a hot climate, rode elephants into battle, and lived along the Indus River. Greeks and Romans of Sima's time wrote of China as the distant land of Seres ("silk"), which they knew was beyond Sindh but which they often left off their maps. By the end of the second century CE, Rome and Han had both made several attempts to send formal embassies, and not merely trade goods or merchant caravans, directly to each other's capitals.

An educated person of the first century CE, living in the right place – Rome, Alexandria, Gandhara, Patna, Chang'an – could acquire a great deal of knowledge about peoples living throughout Eurasia and North Africa, and if healthy and having a certain amount of money could travel thousands of miles to see things in person. Some of our most tantalizing travel reports of this period suggest the long distances that some individuals – primarily merchants and Buddhist religious on pilgrimages – traveled. The Chinese monk Faxian (337–422), for instance, crossed overland from eastern China to southern India, and returned by a coastal journey that took him through Southeast Asia. He left a fairly complete record with a description of the areas he saw. Though not a traveler himself, the Greek geographer Strabo (63 BCE–c.22 CE), one of the best known of these classical geographers, was able to take advantage of the experiences of travelers and of the histories of the Macedonian conquests in northeast India to include a detailed account of Indian cultures in his geographical work.

It is interesting to consider what Strabo made of the cultural differences and similarities he noted between Greeks and Indians. He considers the Indian elites, the Brahmins (Brachmanes to him), to be unappealingly superstitious, and suggests that they are responsible for keeping the majority of Indians living in a physically primitive and politically immature condition. On the other hand, he notes many similarities between the Indians, particularly the Brahmins, and the Greeks. The Brahmins and the Greeks agree that the world was created, and that time has an originating point. They also agree that the world is material, and not eternal. They agree that the world is subject to the control of a superior intelligence. They agree that the earth is round. Both peoples have a concept of primary elements, the most important being water, from which the whole of the material universe is derived (though the details of their systems vary). Both peoples believe in the immortality of the soul, in differing ways accept the doctrine of reincarnation, and also accept that after death the creator of the universe judges the worthiness of the soul to be rewarded or punished.

Today, commentaries on these passages from Strabo point to what we now regard as obvious: The ancient Greeks, the Iranian Bactrians, and the ancient Brahmins shared some cultural heritage through the Indo-European migrations, and the cultural similarities that Strabo noted were evidence of the effects. In addition, Strabo had come upon evidence of what we would call "diffusion," which we will explore in the next chapter of this book. For instance, the idea of judging souls after death was probably an ancient Egyptian idea, which with many other North African influences had some impact in both Greece and in India, thanks to traveling merchants and soldiers.

Strabo had no interest in the origins or meanings of similarities and differences. He found comparisons colorful and expected them to intrigue his readers, but not because they reflected past migrations or cross-cultural influences. Nothing could have been further from his mind than that elements of Greek and Indian culture might have had common roots. The diversity itself was what got his attention, and like his approximate contemporaries in Rome and China he used the differences to stress the ultimate superiority and rationality of his own culture in comparison with those that were subjugated or known only at a distance. He was, in the final analysis, a geographer and an encyclopedist – a scholar of the world as it was, an inquirer in the tradition of Herodotus, a cataloguer of places and peoples. He was not yet a historian, and certainly not a universal historian.

But the contrast of Strabo with Eratosthenes, who lived a century earlier, is illuminating. Greek philosophers before Eratosthenes knew that the earth was round, because the earth casts a circular shadow upon the moon during a lunar eclipse. Eratosthenes, however, wished to know how large a sphere the earth really was. He measured the difference between the length of shadows of objects of the same height at Alexandria and at his home town in North Africa and used the difference in angles to calculate the relationship between real distance and the earth's spherical shape. His educated guess of the earth's size was surprisingly accurate – less than 500 kilometers short. Unlike Strabo, Eratosthenes thought in truly global terms, relating local specifics to universal conditions. And today we remember Strabo primarily for the use he made of Eratosthenes' idea. Like all Greeks, Strabo knew that, because the earth was round, in theory traders should be able to sail westward and eventually reach India, instead of the arduous overland journey that was normally used. In practice his idea could not work at the time, for several reasons. First, the Greeks did not know of the intervening continents of the Americas. Second, Strabo, through an error that has not been explained, thought the world was much smaller than Eratosthenes' more correct estimate, and so he supposed that India was much closer than it was (an error that would persist for many centuries). Nevertheless, Strabo's theory was sound, and would inspire European explorers for many centuries to sail west from the Mediterranean in search of "India." As we know, they ultimately found the West "Indies" and the American "Indians."

During the third through fifth centuries CE, the large empires all disappeared, and were succeeded by new historical narratives and authorities. In Europe, the Middle East, and China, new orders arose – generally smaller in size, showing the strong stamp of local customs, but also determined to claim to any extent possible the heritage of the great empires. In many ways, new histories of classically derived authority were a logical outgrowth of the disintegration of the empires and the emergence of new orders, seeking new legitimacy. In China, multiple empires of various sizes continued the traditions of the Han imperial historians, narrating the missions of their own smaller empires or kingdoms to maintain benevolent government and sustained cultural advancement. Naturally, rival empires within this zone each narrated themselves as the true heirs of the Han, and all their rivals as barbarian impostors.

In this period we see the emergence of a new sort of interest, that of the genealogists of new royalty, who by the nature of their work were necessarily historians. There was perhaps a model for this in claim of the Roman poet (and *de facto* historian) Virgil, that the Trojan prince Aeneas had escaped destruction by the Greeks and eventually became the founder of Rome. In a more sophisticated attempt to create a legitimating narrative, the ruling family of the Tang empire (which would eventually rule a reunited China, after 618 CE), who were largely Turkic in origin, claimed descent from the iconic Chinese philosopher Laozi. But this boast was perhaps outdone by the British historian Nennius, who, writing in the 700s, declared that after Aeneas had founded Rome he had a grandson named Brutus, who eventually went among the Celtic peoples and then on to Britain, which was named for him, as he was the true progenitor of all its rulers, as well as founder of its capital (which according to Nennius was originally called "New Troy").

Writing systems and law were extremely important links, but equally important were narratives explaining the rise of the new rulers, and how they were connected to the elites of the classical period. In China, for instance, the new kingdoms were sometimes ruled by local Chinese, but sometimes by Turks, by Tibetans, or by Sogdian immigrants from the general region of Iran. To justify their right to rule a part of what was once the Han empire, they either learned Chinese or hired Chinese scholars to write and speak for them; they instituted select elements of Han law; they performed some of the old Han imperial rituals; and, most distinctly, they encouraged histories of their peoples showing their connections with the Han empire and with Han elites. Their genealogies, showing their connections to Han officials and nobility if remotely plausible, became the histories of their peoples. It was also important that the writers in these centuries insisted that histories must center on kings and conquests, equating the origins of personal legitimacy for the ruler with national origins. As suggested above, this was not new. But the volume of writing, not only in classical languages but also in vernaculars, was striking.

While the role of Christianity in Europe, and Confucianism in China, and the new religion of Islam in the Middle East, North Africa, and Spain in the legitimation of the post-classical kingdoms and empires is well known, new historical narratives were of equal importance. More relevant to our discussion, these new histories were, unlike the geographies of classical times, eager to explain connections between the present and past, quick to note similarities of names and customs, and to use them to connect peoples distantly related – if related at all – in space and time. Very few of the histories encouraged by these new rulers are now regarded as reliable. However, they represent a very important juncture in the transition from the cataloguing of detail that was characteristic of classical writing all over Eurasia to the understanding of cross-cultural history as a narrative of the sort that classical historians reserved for their own histories of politics and war. These writers of late antiquity and the early medieval period proposed that names, customs, shared myths, and long histories of contact were the elements connecting different peoples in a continuous experience.

An interesting complement to many of his approximate contemporaries, and a harbinger of historical work to come, was Priscus, who was Thracian by birth, given a Greek education, and who worked at the court of the Byzantine emperors in the fifth century. By accompanying ambassadors from the Byzantine court to Egypt and to the courts of the Arab rulers, he became acquainted with many of the cultures bordering Europe. But his most extensive surviving work is his account of his time as ambassador to the court of Attila the Hun (then encamped north of the Black Sea) from 448 to 450. Priscus was a keen and relatively objective observer, used to writing the history of empires and emperors. He rose above the European fear and contempt for the Hunnish invaders to provide an eternally informative description of Attila's life and death, his followers, and the structure of his empire. Most of Priscus' work was lost, but surviving fragments are among our most frequently cited for their vivid and often sympathetic view of a feared enemy. What Priscus could not do, as an official of the Byzantine empire, was to narrate history from the vantage point of the Huns. He could assume a relatively objective view of the Huns, but as a loyal Byzantine official, in the end he had to take the point of view of the Byzantine empire. Nevertheless, in the scope of his experience and the invaluable credibility he gave to his Hunnish informants, Priscus was a forerunner of the medieval historian who eventually accomplished the first self-consciously global history.

In the Middle East and North Africa, the remarkable expansion of Islam in the late 600s and early 700s brought the creation of new, very sophisticated historical work. In Arabic primarily, Islamic scholars wove together the Greek heritage of the western Mediterranean with the history of the nomadic peoples of the Arabian peninsula and the saga of the birth of Islam to generate a sophisticated and influential tradition. Greek techniques of geography and inquiry, Islamic exegetical skills needed for commenting upon the *Qu'ran*, and to a small degree Persian literary traditions all contributed to the flowering of several schools of historical writing, particularly in the eighth and ninth centuries, when the Abbasid empire, based in Baghdad, was at its height.

Abu al-Hasan Ali ibn al-Husayn al-Masudi (896–956), an Abbasid-era Arab historian based in Baghdad, was well aware that he stood on the shoulders of previous historians who had attempted a view of the known world. Like many of his predecessors in the development of Islamic historiography, al-Masudi argued for skepticism and the value of personal opinion in treatment of some religious and scholarly texts. Like Herodotus and Strabo, al-Masudi organized his most influential writing, *Muruj adh-dhahab wa ma'adin al-jawahir* ("The Meadows of Gold and Mines of Gems"), both geographically and chronologically. Like Priscus, he worked his personal observations during travel and residence abroad into his work. In his case, al-Masudi is known to have traveled in Iraq and Iran, the Caucasus, parts of the Mediterranean, parts of northwestern India, and North and East Africa; he may have visited parts of the Byzantine empire as well. From his reading of eighty books, many obviously in Greek, his acquisition of genealogies and diaries while traveling, and his own observation of historical sites, he wove together a composite history of humanity from the time of Abraham to his own time. Europe, China, Africa, India, as well as the Middle East, all figured in his story. His determination to be inclusive and to confirm his details makes him one of our best sources today for some medieval regimes such as the pre-Kievan Rus, the Kazars, the Bulgars, and the early Mamluks. While a distinctive achievement, al-Masudi's feat was primarily a compilation history, not organized around or suggesting major causes or effects of widespread change.

An obvious inspiration behind al-Masudi's inclusive work was the fact that in his time the Abbasid caliphate, or Islamic government, united all the Islamic world, from eastern Iran to Spain. Later, another order unifying distant places would inspire a second, larger attempt at a universal history. In the aftermath of the extraordinary rise and spread of Mongol domination over Eurasia, the historian Rashid al-Din (1247–1318) was the chief civil official of the court of Ghazan, ruler of the Mongol Ilkhans of Persia from 1295 to 1317. Ghazan was a great-grandson of Genghis Khan. In the middle 1200s Mongols under Ghazan's father had swept into Persia and destroyed the former religious government, the Abbasid caliphate, which had been based in Baghdad. Before Ghazan, the Mongol rulers of Persia had not been Muslim, but Ghazan converted to the religion, partly at the urging of Rashid al-Din (who had himself converted to Islam from Judaism at the age of thirty). Under Rashid's influence, Ghazan changed many of the Ilkhan policies in such a way as to relieve tax burdens on the people and allow more freedom to Muslim communities. Ghazan also supported Rashid in completing the first history of the world, a history with a very particular point of view.

In his work *Jami al-tawarikh* ("Compendium of Histories"), Rashid's purpose was not to do anything so formless as recounting all known information about everybody everywhere. He was building on several centuries of historical study by Muslim scholars, including but not limited to al-Masudi, who had devised methods of extracting an early history of the Muslim conquests, and of the life of the Prophet Muhammad, from folk tales and other informal sources. Rashid al-Din had a very clear idea that history had been leading to the conquests and unifying political order of the Mongols, and particularly to the reign of his own patrons, Ghazan and Uljeitu. He believed that under the Mongols all cultural traditions and all religious systems would flourish, with the most righteous (Sunni Islam) eventually gaining ascendancy over the unjust or false. To him, that was the meaning of the past, and from it was derived the meaning of the present and the future.

Apart from sponsored histories of the Mongol regimes, of which Rashid's was the broadest in scope and most ambitious in conception, the Mongol empires of the thirteenth and fourteenth centuries were also noteworthy for producing an extraordinary new wave of travel reports, many of which still have a special place in the study of global history. In the centuries since the Buddhist monk Faxian had traversed most of eastern Eurasia and left his report, many others had undertaken travel and writing of equal scope and importance. The Chinese Buddhist monk Xuanzang had traveled through part of Central Asia, to India and back to China, in the 630s. His account of his journey and adventures became the foundation for an entire genre of Chinese folk and literary entertainments. In the early 900s the Arab traveler Ibn Fadlan wrote a very detailed description of the Varangians, also known as the early Viking founders of Russia, telling of their tales of travel to Iraq, India, and China. In the twelfth century, Benjamin of Tudela traveled from Spain through most of the Islamic Middle East, and left a vivid narrative. After the Mongols established their original capital at Karakorum in Mongolia in 1240, Europeans headed toward the Mongol territories, often hoping to get as far as the court and an audience with the Mongol rulers. Some of these travelers, such as the Venetians Niccolo and Maffeo Polo (father and uncle of Marco), were merchants seeking Mongol permission to continue trade along the lucrative Silk Road. Others were monks, more likely to leave extensive records of their travels. Odoric of Pordenone traveled from Italy to China and back in the 1330s, providing invaluable descriptions of the great cities of Iran, India, island Southeast Asia, the Chinese city of Hangzhou, the Grand Canal, and what is now the city of Beijing in the early days of Mongol occupation.

Odoric was followed a decade afterward – and forever overshadowed by – Giovanni del Pian del Carpine, or John of Plano Carpini, who traveled to Mongolia by way of Kievan Russia and the Central Asian steppe. John's document, which was known in the medieval world in several forms but is conventionally titled *Historia Mongalorum quos nos Tartaros appellamus* ("History of the Mongols, whom we call the Tartars"), was not an incidental description but a careful and thorough analysis of the Mongols and their world, specifically preserving Mongol accounts of their own history. In spirit it owed a bit to Priscus, but it also foreshadowed much of the later work of Rashid al-Din, based as it was upon oral accounts by Mongols and necessarily incorporating their point of view. John of Plano Carpini was one of at least half a dozen European clerics who left accounts of their travels to Asia, but his was by far the best-known account of this period. It was, however, part of a two-way exchange. Rabban Sauma, a Uighur Turk and Nestorian Christian who had been sent by the Mongol rulers to communicate with the European rulers in the late 1280s, visited Constantinople, Rome, Paris, and southern France, and left short but valuable descriptions of the people and their customs.

Among late medieval Europeans, accounts of Asian travel were not only popular but profitable. After Marco Polo accompanied his uncles to China in 1271 and returned to Venice almost twenty-five years later, he and his family staged pageants dramatizing their supposed adventures that drew crowds and contributions, as well as acting as powerful advertising for the family's import-export business. During a period of imprisonment in the late 1290s Marco wrote or dictated his account of his travels, *Il Milione* ("The Million"). It is not an accurate description of China at the time; parts of it are clearly impossible, and the rest could have been learned from other travelers to China, but the book both reinforced the involvement of European seaports in the Eurasian trade network and increased curiosity about the world outside Europe. Not quite a century later the English gentleman John Mandeville would write a popular work claiming to be an account of his travels through North Africa, the Middle East, India, China, and Mongolia. Though Mandeville certainly did a fair amount of traveling, he was probably more widely read than widely travelled, as his account has been shown to be a patchwork of borrowings from classical writers, including Strabo, to genuine medieval travelers, including Odoric of Pordenone and the many histories of the Mongols circulating through Europe in his time. Like Marco Polo, Mandeville played, for fun and profit, upon the European enthusiasm for knowledge of the world.

It was Abu Abdullah Muhammad ibn Battuta (1304–77?) who brought together the best of the trends that had been foreshadowed by Priscus, al-Masudi, Rashid al-Din, and John of Plano Carpini. Unlike any of his predecessors, Ibn Battuta was neither European nor Asian, but African. He was a Berber Muslim scholar from what is now Morocco. In the course of his education and then of his pilgrimages as a devout Sunni Muslim, he traveled through North Africa and the Middle East, and subsequently undertook trade which led him to the rich port towns of East Africa. He later extended his travels to the Byzantine empire, southern Russia, Central Asia and India, Southeast Asia and China. In each of these places, Ibn Battuta sought out informants from the Muslim communities, who told him not only of their own conditions but of the customs and history of the neighboring non-Muslims. In his later life, the sultan of Morocco paid for Ibn Battuta to retire and dictate his travels and observations to a scribe. The resulting work is normally known as the *Rihla*, or *The Travels*. It is a magnificent work, far more reliable and far more extensive in scope than Marco Polo's.

The legacy of Ibn Battuta to modern world historians is a complex one. At the most fundamental level, the written narrative of his travels and investigations is an indispensable example of what is now called "encounter" literature (see chapters 5 and 6). Particularly as the frequency and distance of sea travel increased dramatically in the late fifteenth and sixteenth centuries, individuals of profoundly different cultural traditions began to confront each other in person and often to record their impressions in diaries, letters, or in formal publications afterward. Very soon after Ibn Battuta's travels, for instance, his fellow North African Ibn Khaldun (see chapter 5) used his experience of wide travel to help perfect a major historical interpretation; in the early 1440s, the Chinese traveler Ma Huan – accompanying the Chinese seafarer Zheng He on his Indian Ocean travels – wrote his impression of the cultures and societies of Southeast Asia, India, and the Persian Gulf. A half-century after Ma Huan published his memoirs, the venue for global encounters expanded from the Indian Ocean to southern Africa, the Americas, and to the Pacific. By the middle of the eighteenth century, memoirs of European, Islamic, and Chinese clerics, merchants, soldiers, and officials constituted a rich literature upon which world historians (as well as anthropologists and literary scholars) continue to draw. They are interested not only in the sensations of discovery (though that is valuable in itself), but in the information offered regarding means and routes of travel, the financing of long-distance travel in the new age of regional connectivity, and insights into the concepts that shaped and were shaped by the perceptions of newly met cultures and peoples.

However, Ibn Battuta is a seminal figure for global historians for other reasons. Everywhere he traveled outside North Africa he brought to his observations the perspective of the outsider, the more objective observer. Europeans, Middle Easterners, and Asians were all strangers to him, and he observed them carefully and systematically. On the other hand, Ibn Battuta did not view the world as a riotous confusion of local oddities or bizarre and wondrous worlds (as Marco Polo and John Mandeville had done). As a Muslim, he found that he had immediate grounding in all the regions he visited. He could communicate with locals in the universal Muslim language of standard Arabic and he could participate in at least part of their customs. He could immediately place them in the networks of Muslim belief and education with which he was familiar, and relate the concepts of lineages to people's view of their own identities and histories. For twentieth-century historians coming out of the domination of historical work by national narratives, Ibn Battuta was an important model of a traveler and an observer who saw the world, though vast and diverse, as united by fundamental patterns of trade, cultural influences, migration, religious communities, and historical development. Together with his near-contemporary Ibn Khaldun, Ibn Battuta remains an enduring source for not only the content of global history, but the ideas behind it. By combining the Muslim traditions of historical discipline with his life experiences as a traveler, Ibn Battuta has taught historians afterward how to tame the great story impulse, and harness it to provide new understandings of the structure of human change.

Suggestions for further reading

Bentley, Jerry H., *Old World Encounters: Cross-Cultural Contacts and Exchanges in Pre-Modern Times*. Oxford & London: Oxford University Press, 1993.

Ehret, Christopher, *An African Classical Age: Eastern and Southern Africa in World History, 1000 BC to AD 400*. Charlottesville VA: University of Virginia Press, 2001.

Fernández-Armesto, Felipe, *Pathfinders: A Global History of Exploration*. New York: W. W. Norton, 2006.

Nakamura, Hajime, *Parallel Developments: A Comparative History of Ideas*. New York: Harper & Row, 1975.

Robinson, Chase, *Islamic Historiography*. Cambridge: Cambridge University Press, 2003.

2
Divergence

As we have seen, the earliest narrators of global stories drew upon a basic idea of diffusion in their understanding of human development. They believed that humanity originated at a certain point in space and time, perhaps with a single individual or a pair of individuals, and from there spread out to cover the world. As they moved, they took with them their connections to their god or gods, and also their elaborate kin relationships to each other. As, in the medieval period, literate people all over Eurasia and North Africa became aware of and familiar with vastly expanded frontiers, they were occasionally called upon to account for the strangers as long-lost limbs of the family tree going back to the original founders of the human race. If they could not, then they would be forced, in the style of Marco Polo or John Mandeville, to represent newly encountered peoples as not human – beasts, monsters, or demons.

In the milieu of Europe's "Renaissance" of the sixteenth and seventeenth centuries, the more fanciful notions of the origins of distant peoples were less tolerated, and scholars – many supported by monarchs or by wealthy merchant families doing business in Asia, Africa, or, sometimes, the Americas – set themselves to understanding the more credible sources of diversity in human cultures and economic life. Europeans of the sixteenth and seventeenth centuries tended to try to identify recently encountered peoples of North

America, Africa, and Asia as descendants of individuals or groups mentioned in the Old Testament. Chinese often linked peoples of Northeast and Central Asia to groups mentioned in the records of the Zhou confederacy of the first millennium BCE. By the end of the seventeenth century, both the Europeans and the Chinese had abandoned notions of sub-human or monstrous origins for strangers. Instead, scholars at both ends of Eurasia were attracted to the idea that civilized people (however they might define it) shared a remote origin, which permanently set them apart from barbaric peoples all over the world.

These theories were monogenetic, meaning that they assumed a single origin for all humanity and traced the basic practices that defined civilization back to a single source. From there, the institutions and practices – spoken languages, writing systems, religious ideas, artistic motifs, concepts of the family, and rituals associated with power – were distributed, or diffused, to widely separated places. This theory of diffusionism argued that the diversity of cultures in the world is accounted for by the borrowing, adapting, garbling, and partial loss of the original human culture. Differences arose through local divergences from the original, universal culture.

Where had the original culture developed, and by what means had it diffused? The answers, naturally, depended greatly upon where the historians resided who were doing the telling. Some Japanese scholars of the 1600s, looking at the diversity of religious systems that had reached their country by that time, reconciled their concern over foreign influence with their interest in foreign belief systems by asserting these religions – Buddhism, Christianity and Judaism – had actually originated in Japan, and been diffused from there to other parts of the world. Some Chinese scholars of the eighteenth century argued that Buddhism, the most pervasive religion in China, had originated in China and not in India. But the most elaborate theories were created by European scholars, many of them Jesuits or greatly influenced by Jesuits, in the 1600s and early 1700s. In this period, Jesuits gained a great familiarity with the cultures of East Asia, India, and Southeast Asia and knew well some aspects of the newly discovered cultures of the Americas.

The transition in Jesuit thinking on the relationships of newly discovered peoples to ancient cultures is demonstrated in a comparison of the theories of José de Acosta and Francesco Clavigero. De Acosta visited Mexico in the early years of its conquest by Europeans, and in 1588 wrote a treatise arguing that Mexicans were not humans but were wraiths ruled over by demons controlled by Satan. In the organization of the Mexican priesthood he thought he saw a deliberate satire of the rituals of the Church, a satire in which only Satan could have delighted. More than a century later, Clavigero, who was born in Mexico, wrote a very influential study of the local people (largely Aztec descendants) which argued that the peoples of America were the descendants of Noah. He based this on not only their priestly activities, which he thought resembled those described in the Old Testament, but also their folk traditions, which described destruction of the world by flood. His work, he claimed, was intended to refute notions that the peoples of America had no connection with peoples of Europe, or perhaps only a connection that somehow went back before Adam. All humanity, he argued, had a single genealogical and cultural heritage, even if it dated to the earliest known figures, the heroes of the Old Testament.

In time, ideas like Clavigero's would become the basis of very elaborate speculations, some of them with religious significance, connecting the early American peoples with the "Lost Tribes" of the Jews, who had been abducted by Assyrian forces in the eighth century BCE and then reportedly left for places unknown. In the 1700s, American clergymen and scholars hotly debated the exact relationship of the earlier American populations to migrations narrated in the Old Testament. Some visitors to Central America from Jewish communities in Europe declared that the Lost Tribes had been found. What is striking is that Protestant religious scholars and historians of the 1700s, like their Catholic Jesuit predecessors of the 1600s, refused to accept that humans could have any origin except from Adam and Eve. The medieval theories of demonic, Satanic, or monstrous origins of strange peoples had been permanently set aside.

The fact that, as of about 1600, Europeans recognized a distinct civilization meeting all their criteria – writing, history, law, patriarchy – in China meant that they needed to account for how the institutions of civilization had found their way there. Jesuits and other missionaries of the Catholic Church in East Asia were frequently in tension with the Vatican regarding the degree to which local customs, particularly ancestor worship, should be tolerated in local Christian practice. The missionaries in Asia realized that without a recognition and tolerance of these customs, they were unlikely to make any converts. But the Church insisted that practices it regarded as pagan should not be permitted in Christian observances. In response, Jesuits argued that the Chinese were not alien and barbaric, but that they and their culture descended from the same roots as those of Europe and the Middle East. One of the most energetic and most inventive of the Jesuit researchers was the German Athanasius Kircher. As a boy and a young man Kircher had studied Hebrew and Syriac, as well as Latin. In European libraries of the early 1600s he discovered books on Egyptian history and culture. He learned Coptic, which he argued (correctly) was really a derivative of ancient Egyptian. He then went on to study Egyptian hieroglyphics. He considered these the written form of the original human language spoken by Adam and Eve, and suggested that early alphabets might have been derived from the hieroglyphs (an idea later accepted by scholars). Kircher also had strong interests in geology and meteorology, and was the first known to have plotted and described the Gulf Stream of warm Atlantic waters affecting the coast of North America. Magnetism fascinated him, and he attempted to study its patterns whenever possible, relating to his theory that most major magnetic and geological patterns were connected with the sinking of Atlantis in prehistoric times. Finally, he was an excellent musicologist, leaving an invaluable study of all the musical genres of Europe in his lifetime.

Without going to China, Kircher became interested in the controversies surrounding Chinese culture and religion. He studied Chinese from missionaries who had returned from the country, and learned something of the history not only from the texts available in Europe but also from the inscriptions on monuments reported to him by Jesuits in China. From these sources, and his fertile imagination, Kircher constructed his complete theory of China, its culture, and its writing system. According to him, the Chinese – like the Persians and Central Asians – were descendants of Noah's son Ham. The writing system, in his view, was a derivation and degeneration of Egyptian hieroglyphs and was invented about 300 years after the Flood. As for the culture generally and the religions in particular, Kircher argued that the Chinese, like others in Asia, were descended from the idol-worshiping and magic-practicing peoples named in the Old Testament as the enemies of Abraham, Moses, and the Hebrews. At the same time, they had been influenced by waves of Christian missionaries back to the 600s, and had also been influenced by Buddhism, which Kircher considered a confused and degenerate variation of Christianity. The major figures of Chinese cultural history, such as Fu Xi (the inventor of agriculture and writing) and Kongzi (whose name the Jesuits latinized to Confucius) corresponded to figures known from the very early history of the Middle East, particularly the mysterious inventor of the arts, Hermes Trismegistus. The Chinese, in Kircher's view, were not true barbarians, but were close cousins of civilization. If they were estranged from their European cousins, it was because they had never given up the idolatrous ways that the Hebrew patriarchs and Jesus himself had condemned.

The fact was that Kircher's knowledge of both Egyptian hieroglyphs and Chinese characters was minimal and faulty. His scholarship and that of other Jesuits was given very little respect by scholars of the following two centuries, particularly as some Europeans became more invested in the idea that Asians and Africans were barbarous peoples who were best dealt with through conquest and colonization. Nevertheless, the diffusionist model that he and his contemporaries had adhered to continued to dominate analyses of human history. The idea of far-flung cultural products with a single origin was fundamental to the historical linguists of the nineteenth century who worked out the hypothesis of the "Indo-European" languages. They established, by scientific means that are still accepted generally, that almost all the languages of Europe, as well as such Middle Eastern languages as Hittite and such Central Asian languages as Tokharian, had a single origin. In time, the European scholars working on this came to understand the laws by which sounds and vocabulary had changed, creating the different European languages of the historical era. Some scholars, reconstructing the original language, attempted to describe the natural environment of the Indo-European ancestors. They came up with the idea that the Indo-Europeans had originally lived on the Eurasian steppe, and from there had broken into two groups; one moved gradually southward into Iran and northern India, while the other went westward, conquering and occupying Europe. After more decades of work, they hypothesized that the original population had created the language roughly 5000 years ago.

As late as the 1890s and early twentieth century, the formal "Diffusionist" school was influential in the formation of our modern disciplines of anthropology, sociology, and, of course, "universal" or "global" history. Historical linguistics offered the first objective method for determining patterns of change, allowing the cultural center to be placed both in space and in time (though to the present-day specialists in Indo-European historical linguistics debate the location of the original homeland, placing it somewhere between France and Afghanistan). In Germany and Austria, a group of scholars worked out the idea that in prehistoric times there existed a small set of widely-spaced cultural centers, from which all modern cultures are derived. Besides the Indo-European language group, they acknowledged other language groups across central and northern Eurasia, in East Asia, Southeast Asia, and the Semitic languages of North Africa and the Middle East. For this group of Diffusionists, cultural complexes (*kulturkreise*) of intertwined artistic themes, social organization, and religious practices all corresponded in their patterns of distribution to the large language families with which they were associated, which in turn were produced by migration. One well-known Diffusionist, Wilhelm Schmidt, published a twelve-volume history (finished by 1936) of the concept of God in which he argued that all religions were originally monotheistic, meaning that they saw the world ruled by one supreme god.

These European Diffusionists were in some ways rivaled by a group of Diffusionists in England with a very different notion of how culture evolved and spread. The most famous of these was G. E. Smith, originally an Australian but in 1899 appointed to a fellowship at an Oxford college. In his book *The Migration of Cultures* (1915), Smith argued that all cultures had only one origin: ancient Egypt (Smith's formal academic specialization). The revolution had occurred about 6000 years in the past. Before this transformation, humans had lived without agriculture, clothing, religion, or constructed housing. All writing was derived from Egyptian hieroglyphics; all religions were derived from Egyptian monotheism; all architecture was derived from Egyptian temples and pyramids. Enthusiasm for Smith's ideas was widespread in England in the early twentieth century. Indeed, those ideas were fundamental to H. G. Wells's *Outline of History* (see Introduction above).

To understand the appeal of Smith's idea of "heliolithic diffusion" (in which the culture of the Egypt was reflected through the construction of stone monuments alluding to the worship of a supreme sun deity), it is necessary to consider it in combination with the influence of what is often called "social Darwinism," and with concepts of race at the turn of the twentieth century. Social Darwinism, of course, had very little to do with Darwin's ideas of natural selection. Instead, it was based upon Herbert Spencer's idea of the "survival of the fittest," which hypothesized that history is driven by competition, among animals and among humans; the modern condition of various groups reflects their natural superiority or inferiority in relation to the challenges of nature, and in competition with other groups. Man rules the animals because he is superior to them, and Europeans ruled Asians, Africans, and some Americans because they were superior. Their superiority was encoded in their racial heritage, at the time partly illuminated by the newly discovered principles of genetics. This was materially based, in the view of racial theorists at the beginning of the twentieth century, and could not be changed by history – rather, it changed history. These one-dimensional approaches to history strongly reinforced the methods used by G. E. Smith. As the originators of human culture, the Egyptians had been superior to all their contemporaries. Their most direct heirs had been the Hebrews, the Greeks, and ultimately the Europeans – now all encompassed by the increasingly popular notion of "Western Civilization" being promoted by Oswald Spengler and James Henry Breasted. Other peoples, Smith argued, had received the benefits of Egyptian culture but had misunderstood it, corrupted it, or wasted it. Europeans had caused it to evolve.

Wells himself offered a new dimension to the interpretation in *Outline of History*. He noted that most people in the world were not white or black, but "brunet." The brunet people being the overwhelming majority, they also represent the mainstream. But innovation, change, and advance, Wells argued, always come from the margins. They come from minorities competing to survive and to prosper against the threat from the majority. In his view, this explained most of natural history, and why the most efficient animal predators are never the most numerous species. It also explained human history. The minority – Egyptians, Hebrews, Europeans – had to evolve on the margin to be superior to the majority. They were the source of all innovations. Areas of the world that appeared to have originated agriculture and large-scale architecture on their own (such as the Toltecs of Central America or the Shang dynasty in very early China) were actually outcroppings of Egyptian culture, at much earlier periods than conventional history had acknowledged.

Opposition to English Diffusionism in this early twentieth-century form came from many quarters, based on issues of scientific interpretation and historical data. Anthropologists in the United States could find no evidence for simple diffusionism in America before the European invasions. Europeans were ambivalent about the idea that Egypt was the source of their civilization. Scholars of folklore had noted many basic similarities in mythology from around the world, but tended to explain them as psychological phenomena (partly due to the influence of Freud), or as the general attributes of Paleolithic and Neolithic religions, rather than as diffusionism from an original culture. Nevertheless, English Diffusionism continued to be influential, and in the United States was sponsored by the Yale historian William Graham Sumner. The story that culture had a single origin, and that the Europe and North America were its direct heirs, had a great appeal.

In the middle twentieth century, a good deal of the criticism directed against English Diffusionism did not target the basic idea of a single origin for major cultural and technological breakthroughs, but instead challenged the idea that Egypt, or the early modern and modern "West," was always the source. A pivotal figure in changing these perspectives was Joseph Needham, a chemist and lecturer at Cambridge who in the years just after World War II became interested in China and its scientific history. In his conclusion to *What is History?* in 1961, E. H. Carr commented upon Needham (then still a rather obscure Cambridge researcher) and the implications of his work for a revolution in historical conceptualization and teaching:

> Lectures, I am told, are delivered in this university on the history of Russia and Persia and China – but not by members of the faculty of history. The conviction expressed by professor of Chinese [E.G. Pulleyblank] in his inaugural lecture five years ago that "China cannot be regarded as outside the mainstream of human history" has fallen on deaf ears among Cambridge historians. What may well be regarded in the future as the greatest historical work produced in Cambridge during the past decade has been written entirely outside the history department, and without any assistance from it: I refer to Dr. Needham's *Science and Civilization* [sic] *in China*. This is a sobering thought.[1]

Carr may have been right in his assessment of the stature of Needham's work. Despite Needham's death in 1995, new volumes of his *Science and Civilisation in China* (the first volume of which appeared in 1954) continue to appear, and others originally designed for the project have grown into independent articles and monographs. Though to many readers the sprawling work appears to be primarily encyclopedic – an attempt to record all information available on the topics of science and technology in Chinese history – in fact Needham's own analyses of his and other scholars' contributions to the work reveal that his fundamental historical concern with the ideas of diffusion. He saw that the evidence disproved the assumption that all scientific knowledge and technological innovation was to be traced to Europe or to its antecedents in Egypt. In Needham's view, the evidence compelled a different diffusionist model altogether, one in

1 *What is History?*, pp. 146–7.

which China was the source of technological innovation and scientific insight, which diffused from there westward to India, the Middle East, and Europe. Needham did not insist that China was the single source of innovation, but in his view China had contributed the overwhelming majority of pre-modern technologies. He argued that in their philosophical outlook the early Chinese were naturalistic and rational, which allowed them to make strides in mathematics, astronomy, geology, chemistry, and pharmacology when most of the rest of the world was still mired in superstition. The result had been Chinese leadership in paper-making, shipbuilding, compass-making, map-making, clock-making, earthquake-resistant engineering, high-heat metallurgy, waterwheels and mills, windmills, steam-operated engines to run looms and threshers, and many other technologies to mechanize some industries when Europe was still in the "Dark Ages" and the Middle East engulfed in the wars of Muslim expansion. The means by which the technologies spread appeared also easy to confirm: the Silk Road routes that had been active back to the time of the Egyptian pharaohs, and the Indian Ocean sea routes that the Chinese had been exploring a thousand years before Europeans arrived there. The diffusion, Needham argued, had gone from East to West, not from West to East.

The most famous reverse-diffusion experiment of the twentieth century had something in common with the spirit of Needham's project. This was the *Kon-Tiki* expedition of Norwegian zoologist Thor Heyerdahl in 1947. Heyerdahl knew of the work of diffusionists such as W. H. R. Rivers (a mentor of G. E. Smith but clearly not a sympathizer with his Egypt-only model). Among the cultural complexes proposed by Rivers and others was one centered on Java and Southeast Asia, explaining the origins of the peoples who had explored and settled the Pacific. They saw the Pacific Islands as divided into three large regions – Micronesia, Melanesia, and Polynesia. The settlement of the Pacific had in their view proceeded from west to east, with Micronesia settled first, Melanesia next, and finally Polynesia, the easternmost region encompassing a triangle with its points at Hawaii, New Zealand, and Rapanui (then commonly called Easter Island). Their analysis of the development and relationship of the languages of the Pacific paralleled this. Heyerdahl and others were not convinced.

Heyerdahl speculated that settlement of the Pacific might well have happened in the opposite direction. Populations related to early Americans could have started in Rapanui and proceeded westward, taking with them crops such as the sweet potato that were common in Polynesia but known to be of American origin. Heyerdahl invoked legends of Rapanui and some other Polynesian islands together with accounts of early European expeditions to the Pacific describing "white" or fair-skinned peoples to theorize that Polynesia and perhaps even the western Pacific had first been settled by people who originated in the vicinity of Peru, who used balsa wood rafts and brought with them crops, the technologies of agriculture, and a religion of peace. In time they had been overrun by warlike peoples from the west, but the legacy of the original inhabitants had endured.

An argument against Heyerdahl's hypothesis was that early Americans had not been seafarers. Their boats, most scholars assured him, had been suitable for river travel and for moving along the coasts, but could not have covered the distances for Pacific discovery. Heyerdahl and his crew reconstructed an Incan raft as described by the first European visitors, and attempted to sail it westward across the Pacific. Contrary to all expectations they covered 4300 miles in 101 days, finally beaching the *Kon-Tiki* in the Tuamoto Islands. The achievement was spectacular, and was one of many developments changing our perceptions of how mobile ancient peoples may have been – a realization that has been important in very recent theories of how peoples of various parts of eastern Asia might have settled the Americas. In subsequent expeditions, Heyerdahl challenged other cultural complexes cherished by the European Diffusionists. In one, he showed that ancient Africans were physically capable of crossing the Atlantic to the Americas. A later experiment intending to show the practicality of sea travel from the Middle East to the Indus Valley (where European Diffusionists saw a distinct, autonomous root civilization) 4000 years ago was frustrated by war in the Persian Gulf in 1978.

Heyerdahl's adventures were very dramatic and inspired world-wide enthusiasm for anthropology, world history, and alternative historical theories. His ideas about the peopling of the Pacific, however, were eventually disproved by a new science of diffusion, that of genetic mapping. On the basis of this we now know that the Pacific was settled by peoples first living in Taiwan, and subsequently migrating both to Southeast Asia and across the Pacific. This approach (though not the Taiwan finding, which is more recent) was first used prominently in the work of Luigi Cavalli-Sforza, a geneticist who expanded his interests to linguistics, anthropology, and migration history. In the 1960s gene mapping and close analysis of any genetic traits were not possible. However, Cavalli-Sforza and his team first worked with blood types to determine possible patterns of ancestral connections among modern populations. In subsequent decades (their masterwork, *Genes, Peoples and Languages*, was published in 2001), they were able to apply fundamental elements of DNA research to their work. At the same time, they incorporated data on language, surnames, and culture to build a new perspective on human origins and dispersal.

Cavalli-Sforza and his team's basic findings corresponded with and appeared to confirm the general conclusions then current in anthropology, where they had been proposed on the basis of research into bones and living sites. According to the geneticists on Cavalli-Sforza's team, humans had originated in Africa. About 60,000–70,000 years ago, a migration out of Africa had taken people through the Middle East into Asia, and then on to Australia. About 40,000 years ago, modern humans had migrated from the Middle East into Europe, killing off or starving out the last of the Neanderthals. About 20,000 years before, humans had migrated from Northeast Asia into the Americas, completing the global peopling process. Research on contemporary populations revealed no truly isolated populations; on the contrary, all humans are virtually identical genetically, with only small variations that allow the tagging of individual ancestors. On the basis of such tags, migrated groups – Asians or Africans in America, Indians or Iranians in Central Asia – could be linked to their specific regions of origin, not merely to geo-political national entities. Perhaps most provocatively, Cavalli-Sforza and his collaborators proposed a theory of "dual-inheritance" to explain why their work applied not only to genes but to human history generally. Gene movement and cultural development, they proposed, proceed together. When peoples mutually trade goods, technologies, or religions, they also choose marriage or sex partners from newly encountered groups. According to this understanding, no culturally significant exchanges can occur without leaving their traces in the gene pools of both cultures.

With the completion of human genome mapping in 2003, it would now appear possible to solve all questions about the movement and increase (or extinction) of particular groups over the entire expanse of human history. Using mother-transmitted mitochondrial DNA, researchers at the University of California, Berkeley, announced they had discovered that all humans are descended from a woman who lived in East Africa about 140,000 years ago. In time, the descendants of this "Eve" displaced the descendants of other females who had lived during her time. In waves of migration – probably repeated migration out of East Africa in all directions – this genetic strain gained ascendancy. Subsequently, Eve's descendants carried on the process of diffusion and diversification. In other research, studies of the Y-chromosome that determines male sex suggested that all living men (in 2001) descended from a single male ancestor ("Adam," of course) who lived about 50,000 to 100,000 years ago. In 2004, research suggested, after some adjustments made in computer modeling, that all living people may have a common ancestor living as recently as a few thousand years ago, probably in eastern Eurasia. Other research traced the descendants of individuals such as Genghis Khan, supposedly an ancestor of twelve million men in various parts of the world, though overwhelmingly Asian; new projects are under design to trace living populations to other men who probably have a great number of descendants, for example Moses, Edward I of England, Charlemagne, and Giocangga (grandfather of Nurgaci, founder of the Qing empire).

Nevertheless, the research seems to raise many new questions. Critics of Cavalli-Sforza's work have increased in recent years, and critics of new gene studies of the past have always been active. For one thing, a close understanding of the rate of gene change is necessary to make the findings historically significant. It is important to know whether "Eve" lived

20,000 years ago or 200,000 years ago or two million years ago. Much closer dating would be more useful, and an improvement on what anthropology already offers. Yet geneticists do not agree on the rate of change or what environmental factors affect it. This applies especially to the micro environment of the genes themselves, which are complexly influenced in their activity and transmission by the surrounding chromosomes, oncogenes, and proteins, as well as the presence of other genes. Even mitochondrial DNA, in some ways the simplest genetic element to research and to analyze, continues to reveal new complexities in its behavior. Related to this is the issue of what many geneticists call "junk" DNA (residual DNA that appears to have lost its ability to affect the physical body, and as a consequence would not be influenced by environmental factors that would force the loss or mutation of some genes for the lineage to survive); exactly what genes are "junk," and how this affects their significance for understanding human genetic change over time, is still open to dispute.

More critical in some ways have been doubts about the concepts used to analyze, publish, and teach the Cavalli-Sforza results. The vast majority of geneticists (including Cavalli-Sforza) have emphasized that there is no scientific basis for a concept of "race" (meaning in this instance, stable, comprehensive, and categorical differences between groups of humans), and so much less a scientific basis for "national" identities. Yet, in his publications he and his team normally use racial and national terms to describe their populations. This raises the question of circular reasoning. If the group began seeking to compare "English" and "Danish" populations, for instance, or to compare "Europeans" to "Africans," and found no meaningful differences, but then report the results as pertaining to "English" or "Danish" or "European" or "African," how meaningful is the research and how much does its publication advance our notions of the structure of human experience and identity? Anthropologists and historians of culture would respond that racial and national categories are obviously not objective, but are "social constructions" – controlled by the general patterns of group thinking and public expression. As such, they are objects of study in themselves, not the framework for expressing new scientific findings. For population geneticists such as those working in the Cavalli-Sforza mode, making a contribution beyond what anthropologists and cultural historians have already surmised would seem to require transcending the ideologically charged and a priori subjective vocabulary of race and nationality.

For instance, despite the fact that most physicians in the United States have been taught that sickle-cell anemia is a disease of "African-Americans," the genetic research shows that it actually affects and defines an ancestral population encompassing the Mediterranean and Northeast Africa; "Italians," "Lebanese," and others descended from early inhabitants of this zone may also be affected. We have no common word to describe this world, either genetically or culturally (for according to Cavalli-Sforza's "dual-inheritance" theory, genes and culture should be at least overlapping if not identical). On the other hand, population geneticists working not with nations but with geographically distinct locations – such as Britain, including Scotland and Wales – have been able to change our view of history. In the case of Britain, they have discovered that despite the historical narratives of large migrations, first Celtic, then Saxon, then Norman, changing the island and its people, the fact is that the population is genetically the same as it was 9000 years ago; the great conquests have had remarkable cultural and political effects, but they have not significantly changed the genetics of Britain. But in China, genetic research has suggested the contrary case. In a study originally published in 2000 but revisited and re-analyzed several times since, an international team found that the population of northeastern China (specifically Shandong province) had changed substantially between 2500 years ago and 2000 years ago, and changed again significantly between 2000 years ago and the present. In contrast to the history of Britain, Chinese history has tended to emphasize continuity of culture and genealogy. But population genetics suggest that the political and cultural continuities of China may have taken place despite marked differences in the ancestry of the population. Such revelations, though very much in the spirit of the Cavalli-Sforza team's methods, nevertheless contradict their general interpretations. Particularly susceptible to criticism is the "dual-inheritance" principle; skeptics contend that cultural and technological influence can take place separately from migration, contrary to Cavalli-Sforza's hypotheses. In the case of Britain and China, this certainly seems to have been the case.

Nevertheless, the work of population geneticists as a group illustrates an important truth of diffusionist explanations in global history. Some simplistic diffusionist arguments, such as those of G. E. Smith and H. G. Wells, are easily disproved. But the more sophisticated diffusionism of the European school, with its idea of cultural complexes expanding through migration in ancient times and eventually contacting and influencing each other, remains fundamental to our ways of understanding and – perhaps equally important – narrating global history. The cultural complexes made influential by W. H. R. Rivers may have been necessary for us to begin to understand global history, but they were not sufficient. Some cultural systems have a diffusion history of their own – such as the formal religions of Buddhism, Christianity, and Islam – that do not correspond closely to the diffusion of language groups or genetic populations. The same can be said for the spread of early technologies relating to metallurgy, to the horse and chariot, or to stringed musical instruments, to cite miscellaneous examples. In the nineteenth, twentieth and twenty-first centuries, rapid long-distance transport together with cable, wireless, and satellite communications have produced channels of influence and cultural change that transcend language, religion, and genetics.

At each step, challengers of basic diffusionist dogma such as Needham and even Heyerdahl have forced more complexity and multidimensionality into our understandings of cultural spread and change. Yet, disproving a standing hypothesis does not mean that the new hypothesis is true. Heyerdahl's vivid demonstration of the physical possibilities of long-distance travel in ancient times was thought-provoking, but later linguistic and genetic research demonstrated that his ideas about the settlement of the Pacific were wrong. In the case of Needham's history of gunpowder, we now know that it was not a Chinese invention. Monks from the vicinity of modern Afghanistan brought the formula for an early, mildly explosive mixture with them to China, probably in the

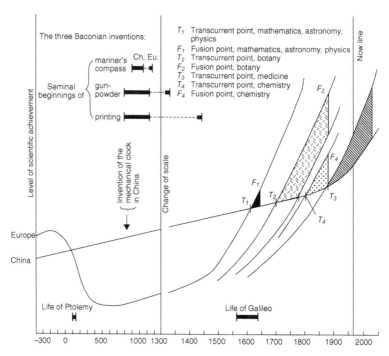

Figure 1 Needham's graph of the time differences between China and Europe in the possession of key technologies, showing a steady increase on the part of China and a sharp decline after the dissolution of the Roman empire, followed by rapid uptick in Europe after the importation of Chinese knowledge. *Source:* Needham, *Clerks and Craftsmen in China and the West,* p. 414.

sixth century. It was useful in controlling mosquitoes and other disease-carrying insects and helped Chinese settlers move into what is now south China, where they largely displaced the original inhabitants. Subsequently, Chinese scholars and soldiers learned to increase the explosive properties of the formula, using it for fireworks and for warfare. The development of guns necessary to take full advantage of its military potential was a winding story of Chinese, Mongol, Persian, and European participation. Others of Needham's claims for originality and exclusivity in Chinese inventiveness have also been shown to be exaggerated. What is important is that Needham showed that Europe had no monopoly on scientific interest, insight, or achievement. China was a major factor, and later scholars, particularly Marshall Hodgson (see chapter 6) have shown the very powerful role of medieval Islamic scholars in the development of mathematics, astronomy, and medicine. Others have demonstrated a fundamental role for South Asia in mathematics, and we are only beginning to understand the achievements of Central American mathematics and astronomy long before the arrival of Europeans.

In the case of population genetics research, the basic diffusionist paradigm is unavoidable: the overwhelming majority of anthropologists, archeologists, historians, and geneticists agree that humanity, as early modern scholars such as Clavigero foresaw, has a single origin. The evidence from all quarters suggests it was in East Africa. From there, it seems that a very complex history of successive migrations and displacement of earlier populations over much more than a hundred thousand years produced the current genetic homogeneity of modern humans. There is far more to be understood, including finding out what the complex genetic history of the bacteria that have been evolving inside us, along with us, can tell. It will be a long time before this story is completely understood, before the basic genetic patterns that lie far under our superficial and ephemeral notions of "race" and "ethnicity" are both known and able to be narrated sensibly. Though diffusionism has been qualified and sculpted to fit the continuous learning of historians, it can never be discarded as a fundamental tool for understanding and narrating the human past.

Suggestions for further reading

Blaut, James M., *The Colonizer's Model of the World: Geographical Diffusionism and Eurocentric History*. New York: Guilford Press, 1993.

Cavalli-Sforza, Luigi Luca and Francesco Cavalli-Sforza, *The Great Human Diasporas: The History of Diversity and Evolution*. New York: Addison-Wesley, 1995.

Cipolla, Carlo, *Guns, Sails and Empires: Technological Innovation and the Early Phases of European Expansion 1400–1700*. New York: Minerva Press, 1965.

Kristiansen, Kristian and Michael Rowlands, *Social Transformation in Archaeology: Global and Local Perspectives*. London: Taylor & Francis (Routledge), 1998.

Renfrew, Colin, *Systems Collapse as Social Transformation: Approaches to Social Archaeology*. Edinburgh: Edinburgh University Press, 1984.

3
Convergence

In the last chapter we saw how the story of a single origin for humanity, using distance and localization to explain modern cultural and technological differences, became an important tool for understanding and telling global history. Historians of early modern and modern times began to develop a second primary theme in global narrative, that of convergence: the idea that over time differences between even widely separated peoples will begin to be displaced by increasing similarity. These similarities can have two general explanations. The first, which we already encountered in discussion of diffusion, is direct or indirect influence, which may explain the adoption of some ideas or beliefs, customs, technologies, loan words, and artistic styles. Far more comprehensive is the idea of developmental paradigms – the hypothesis that all peoples pass through distinct stages of development, and will all end up at the same terminal point in their historical journeys whether or not they come into contact. At the same time that G. E. Smith was working on diffusionist explanations for cultural similarities, other ethnologists and anthropologists, foremost among them James Frazer, were using convergent ideas of cultural universalism and Darwinism to argue that all cultures go through the same basic stages of development. In Frazer's *The Golden Bough: A Study in Magic and Religion* (1890) and his later studies building on it, an early magical culture or totemic worship and sacrifice that would eventually be superseded by rational culture and finally by scientism left traces on the folklore, religious concepts, and historical narratives of all peoples. In the early twentieth century, Sigmund Freud also applied his ideas of personal psychological conflict to folk narratives and universal stages of cultural development, in his *Totem and Taboo: Resemblances between the Mental Lives of Savages and Neurotics* (1913). These works are no longer claimed by global or universal historians as their heritage, and are regarded as more relevant to anthropologists and scholars of literary theory. But they were integral to the transition in the thinking of global historians from simple diffusionist concepts to theories of universal historical staging, leading to parallel and increasingly similar development of independent societies.

A great problem for global historians has been accounting for the origins of agriculture. This was never successfully explained through diffusion, but later became essential to paradigm theories of human development. Many thinkers regarded the idea of agriculture as one of the objective stages through which humanity inevitably passes, regardless of culture or geography. Greek and Roman philosophers had speculated about this, assuming that speech and agriculture might have been related, since social organization was necessary to agriculture and speech was necessary to social organization. Chinese philosophers contemporary with the Greeks and Romans thought that political authority and agriculture were related. They saw innovation and leadership as requirements for agriculture and so argued that early people must have had political leaders in order to become farmers. Medieval European religious writers implied that as an expression of God's love of man, nature is spontaneously abundant and man was an agriculturalist by virtue of his creation by God. With the Renaissance in Europe, thinkers about the past returned to the Greek and Roman speculations about the interplay of the natural environment, human nature, and agriculture. But in their view, agriculture was not the beginning of civilization. It marked a crude stage in human development, and its continued practice by independent families working the land (as contrasted to large, proto-industrial plantations) was a residual sea of barbarism on which twinkled the bright islands of cities, universities, courts, cathedrals, and other upwellings of civilization. In eighteenth-century Europe, the French mathematician and philosopher Jean-Antoine-Nicolas de Caritat, Marquis de Condorcet, argued that the transition to agriculture was one of the universalist stages in the development of humanity during which would continue the drive for deeper science, better technologies, and the universal liberation of all races and genders (a philosophy of history later known in England as "Whiggism.") In the nineteenth century, historians and archeologists attempting to understand the origins of agriculture thought briefly in terms of a diffusionist model – that agriculture had originated in Egypt or the ancient Middle East, and knowledge of it had then spread to other parts of Eurasia and eventually to the world.

These assumptions regarding agriculture were rarely challenged until the mid-twentieth century. Research has now shown that agriculture has multiple origins. We have archeological evidence of people grinding grains and baking bread in the general region of the eastern Mediterranean and south of the Black Sea over 20,000 years ago, well before evidence of agriculture. Most likely, people cooked and baked with wild grains long before learning to grow and harvest them. The earliest evidence of successful, organized agriculture comes from what is modern-day Iraq, where it appears that wheat was a staple crop nearly 10,000 years ago. It is possible that within only a thousand years after this, agriculture had also appeared independently in northern China, in the region of the Amazon River, and in Southeast Asian/Pacific islands such as Papua New Guinea. The Harappan civilization of northern India was growing wheat and barley no later than 7000 years ago. The Anatolian region of what is now modern Turkey as well as the region of modern Egypt, Sudan, and Ethiopia in East Africa had established wheat agriculture by about a thousand years after that. Rice-growing appeared in part of what is now Thailand about 7000 years ago. To make the picture more complex, farmers in what is now Mexico, Guatemala, and Honduras were developing their own agriculture, with their distinct crop of corn (maize) by about 6000 years ago, and within possibly a few hundred years there were new, independent agricultural zones developing along the east coast of North America and in the Andes Mountains. And in Africa, the growing of millet and sorghum was widespread throughout the central and northern regions, including the area of the present-day Sahara, before it became a desert.

If this profound change in the lives of people all over the world between about 9000 and 5000 years ago could not be explained by a diffusionist model, what did explain it? Until the mid-twentieth century, historians assumed that the transition to agriculture was explained by mankind's instinct for comfort, security, and wealth. Humans, in this view, would naturally assume that harvesting grain from dense fields was better than foraging through forests and meadows to gather a handful at a time. However, the intense water management and labor needed for the transition would require some degree of social organization already in place. Human groups without significant population growth, or without stratification of status and authority, could not become agricultural on their own. The historian Karl Wittfogel, writing just after World War II, saw the key to the transition to agriculture as the presence of very large rivers that could supply water necessary for irrigation. He pointed to the Euphrates and Tigris rivers in ancient Iraq, to the Nile in Egypt, to the Yellow River in China and to the Indus in northern India as explaining the very early emergence in those areas of both agriculture and complex societies, a pattern he described as "oriental despotism." To harness the rivers' resources while protecting themselves from floods, these cultures had developed early, centralized states with absolute power over the population at large. They could organize the labor necessary to build dams and dykes, irrigation channels, wells, and drainage systems, while forcing the majority of people to work as slaves or virtual slaves in the fields. The elites of such societies, Wittfogel claimed, had created the foundations of our religions, writing systems, and legal systems; an abundance of food their populations had grown provided them with both motive and means to embark upon wars of conquest against their neighbors, producing the world's first empires. Wittfogel also speculated that these long and deep traditions of authoritarian government had produced political traditions in the Middle East and Asia that contrasted to the democratically minded cultures of Europe and North America.

Though a stimulating argument that seemed to explain broad elements of the past and the present, Wittfogel's thesis does not match well our current understanding of the transition to agriculture. Some early centers of farming, such as eastern Africa and the Andes mountains of South America, do not appear to have been centered upon a major river. In other cases, as in the early Amazon and Mekong river basins, or Anatolia, North America, and Melanesia, the establishment of agriculture was not accompanied by the appearance of large, despotic states with imperial ambitions. And it is not sufficient to say that wherever humans could make the change to agriculture they did it as an obvious or natural thing. We now know that the transition to agriculture was, in many cases, traumatic. Unstable crops or bad weather produced frequent calamities, and for hundreds of years people living in early agricultural zones experienced malnutrition, with the result of a diminution in body size, life expectancy, and infant survival as well as the appearance of diseases of dietary deficiency, such as rickets. Far from explaining agriculture by claiming that it was an attractive and obvious solution, it may now be necessary to explain the transition to agriculture as happening despite the physical suffering, insecurities, and massive labor that it required. We now know that, on the eve of agriculture, hunters and gatherers were healthy, had excellent knowledge of plants to be used for nutrition and for healing, and had a good deal of personal freedom in small and fairly flexible social groups. Why would they give it all up to become farmers?

Social scientists have still not found an explanation that is satisfactory to all, and it appears that convincing explanations will have to take into account not only humans themselves but a full history of the environment. Clearly, climate was a factor. The earliest agriculture centers emerged soon after the end of the last Ice Age about 10,000 ago, which suggests that humans undertook some form of agriculture promptly when climate change made it possible. That only explains why agriculture did not happen earlier, not why it happened at all. But the rapidity of climate change in the period of about 10,000 to 9000 years ago may help explain some things. This is the essential idea behind Kent Flannery's "Broad Spectrum Revolution" thesis. In his view, the environmental changes stimulated by the warming of the earth led to a much greater variety of plants available for both humans and animals to eat, resulting in more human consumption of both vegetables and meat. This greater variety of plant life meant that not only was the human travel range widened, but the population grew significantly too. Increased interest in and knowledge of plants combined with the increasing population and new attachment to good dwelling places, producing both the motivation and opportunity to experiment with controlled cultivation of plants – particularly those grasses, or cereals, that in various forms were related to the modern strains of wheat, rice, and corn – whose life cycles were already well known.

In this view, the domestication of plants was a parallel to the domestication of animals, which happened at least as early as farming and in most places a bit earlier. Hunters realized after some time that certain animals would adapt to life in enclosures, where it would be easier than in the open forests to capture them for butchering. Grazing animals, such as the wild ancestors of cattle and sheep, were particularly suitable as they were attracted to clearings near human habitation and did not feel the need to roam about if grass was underfoot. Modern environmentalists would add that the theory will not be persuasive until it includes the element of "co-evolution": Not only humans were ready for the transition to the domestication of plants and animals, but certain plants and animals improved the survival chances of their species if they entered into a domestication arrangement with people.

Whatever explanation for the agriculture puzzle will eventually be found, the transition to agriculture is the primary fact in human cultural diversity, and it has no diffusionist explanation. It marked, first, the dividing line between the Paleolithic age of hunting and gathering and the Neolithic period of farming, towns, and complex hierarchical societies. It also differentiated agriculturalists from hunter-gatherers, the small minority of people, some still living, who never experienced agriculture at all. It further divided the world between those directly or indirectly involved in agriculture and those who related symbiotically to the agriculture zones as pastoralists or nomads. Successful, intensive agriculture underlay the spectacular growth of population in areas such as northern India, China, and Central America that has continued from prehistoric times to the present. These farming societies built civilizations based upon their crop choices, their irrigation resources and techniques, their labor patterns, their methods of dividing the harvests, the relationships they established between labor in the fields and land ownership. Most developed writing systems for keeping records and mathematics for analyzing their crops and their economies. They learned the sciences of astronomy, calendar-making and meteorology to understand where each day stood in the annual cycle of seasons. They consolidated religious beliefs, sacred texts, and priestly ranks to assure the fertility of the fields. They bred new varieties of dogs, specially suited to the specific tasks needed to manage their farming tasks. In contrast to Paleolithic times, when most humans had the same general economy of hunting and gathering and the same general culture of shamanism and small-group survival, Neolithic humanity was a complex mixture of densely populated agricultural zones, sparsely populated pastoral ranges, different languages, religions, writing systems, and some highly centralized states bent upon conquest and exploitation of neighbors.

Many explanations have been offered for understanding the full range of cultural, social, and material changes in human life since the beginning of the agricultural era. One of the most influential, and comprehensive, was that offered by American ethnologist Lewis Henry Morgan, who published *Ancient Society* in 1877. Morgan was a student of the social history of American Indian groups and of the natural history of North America. He thought that the variety of technological and social patterns to be observed among North American native peoples in the nineteenth century was a living laboratory for understanding general human development. His method was largely what we would now call comparative – comparing the Iroquois and the ancient Greeks, the Aztecs and the Romans, the Maya and the Turks. He deduced a universal paradigm of human development (the stages of which he referred to as "ethnical periods"). Altogether he marked out six phases of development before the "status of civilization." Transition from the first to the second was marked by the discovery of fire and the practice of fishing; from the second to the third by invention of the bow and arrow for hunting; from the third to the fourth by knowledge of pottery; from the fourth to the fifth by domestication of animals in Africa and Eurasia and by the domestication of corn in America; from the fifth to the sixth by the smelting of iron; "civilization" (Morgan's final stage) began with the use of phonetic alphabets. Across time periods Morgan traced what he regarded as the seven great human institutions: subsistence, the family, government, language, religion, housing and architecture, and property. Government, he thought, had its origins in the domination of the majority by elite lineages long before agriculture was introduced. The family was a by-product of elite lineage organization, formed from interaction with new practices of property definition and disposition. Housing grew from the development of the family. And although property, particularly private property, was an obscure theme in much of human history, its conceptual and legal crystallization was the spark that dispelled the darkness of barbarism: "Its dominance as passion over all other passions marks the commencement of civilization. It not only led mankind to overcome the obstacles which delayed civilization, but to establish political society on the basis of territory and property."[1]

Soon after publication of *Ancient Society*, the European social philosopher Friedrich Engels incorporated some of its ideas in his book *The Origin of the Family, Private Property and the State* (1884). Engels was already well known as the co-author with Karl Marx of *The Communist Manifesto* in 1848, and after years of political turmoil in Europe forced both Marx and Engels to settle in England in the 1850s, Engels became an important financial and intellectual support for Marx. Though he later wrote out his own theories about human evolution and the origins of society, state, and religion, Engels was also a direct influence on Marx during the years when the latter worked out what is perhaps the single most influential convergence understanding of human history. In his youth Marx had been a follower of the German idealist philosopher Georg W. F. Hegel. Today Hegel's thought is often simplified almost beyond recognition, but in relation to

1   Morgan, *Ancient Society*, ch. 1, "Ethnical Periods," p. 6.

historical study it is unavoidable that we attribute to him the idea of "dialecticism."

Put briefly, Hegel saw all aspects of both historical development and the human consciousness of history as produced by interaction between the present and the past itself. Large historical processes such as imperialism or industrialization will at any point in time come into conflict with ongoing human aspirations (of particular interest to Hegel, a hypothesized human desire for freedom). These conflicts, or "contradictions," will produce changed circumstances, which over time will lead to new conflicts and new resolutions. The whole process is sometimes reduced to the terms "thesis" (meaning conditions or awareness produced by the past), "antithesis" (meaning the challenges presented to the thesis by human dissatisfactions), and "synthesis" (meaning the new situation arising from temporary resolution of the contradictions). Marx thought the overall idea of dialectical change was persuasive, but he rejected the idealism of Hegel's conviction that a universal mind was somehow controlling history by manifesting itself in nations, laws, and arts. Marx's opposing view is often called "dialectical materialism" – the hypothesis that physical conditions in human social, economic, and political life produce the contradictions that lead to major transformative stages in historical development. The precise point of contradiction in any historical society that leads to transformation is what Marx called the "relations of production," by which he meant, primarily, the organization of society into social classes, each of which induces its individual members to make certain basic assumptions about their roles in work and in reward.

Marx, with influence from Engels, first outlined his stages of history in 1859, and developed it in various essays and books until his death in 1883 (after which Engels continued to extend the various ideas to an explanation of human prehistory). On the basis of work by contemporary German philosophers and archeologists, Marx and Engels believed that the earliest Germans had been "tribal," by which they meant that they had owned no private property and each member of the tribe (combinations of lineages of equal status) enjoyed the proceeds of hunting and gathering forays. Engels later came to believe that this hypothesis, generalized to all humanity, was confirmed by Morgan's study of Native American societies. In this tribal scenario there had been no important contradictions except those produced by the elites of some lineages, who learned to distort the original relations of production in such a way as to collect increasing goods and food for themselves and their kin, while diminishing the rewards and the status of the majority. These changes in social formation together with the transition to agriculture, Marx and Engels hypothesized, had produced what they described as the early slave societies. At first Marx and Engels, inspired by the ideas of European scholars at the time, assumed that a particular "mode of production" based upon slave agriculture had taken long-term root in the Middle East, India, and China, but they eventually moved away from this to a more universal mode of historical transformation.

Slave societies, Marx and Engels hypothesized, were characterized by a dynamic that on the one hand kept degrading the physical well-being of the enslaved majority, making them eventually prone to revolt; on the other hand it produced a class of empowered supporters, who defined their interests separate from those of the ruler. The result was a new age of feudalism, in which a decentralized aristocratic, or noble, class controlled the distribution of land rights, wealth, power, status, security, and education through hierarchical reciprocal relations among themselves, while the majority farming population worked land that they did not own in return for sustenance and protection provided by the aristocrats. Over time, Marx and Engels thought, the rise of special arts and crafts, as well as more profitable kinds of agriculture, would create new concentrations of wealth among merchants, some farmers, and artisans. This would lead to new forms of private ownership, new urban classes, new forms of status, and a general dissolution of the old social and cultural bonds that kept feudalism in place. Instead, history would move on to its capitalist, or bourgeois, stage. Private ownership of land and factories would produce wealth that in itself would be transforming – through banking, through investment in new enterprises and in machinery to make them more efficient, through the consolidation of wealth in larger corporations and through family connections. In its early stages private ownership would be widespread, producing independent farmers and many small, personally owned and run businesses. But over time, the drive for greater profit, efficiency, and mechanization would consolidate wealth in the upper classes, and reduce ownership and income among laborers. Final contradictions between this system of greater wealth at the top and more poverty at the bottom would eventually produce revolutions that would usher in a socialist period, in which the majority of workers would enjoy leverage through organizations such as labor unions and popular education clubs to ensure their well-being in an industrialized and still stratified world. Through the progressive action of this majority, Marx and Engels foresaw a final stage of communism, in which all individuals enjoyed the same status, the same access to the proceeds of their labor, as had our original human ancestors.

The precise means by which Marx and Engels explained the transition from one stage to another, as well as the contradictions that compelled those transitions, were complex and changed somewhat between 1859 and Engels' death in 1895; many of them were developed by later writers, some of whom we will review in chapter 5. They believed that they lived in the capitalist or bourgeois period, but that the age of socialist transformation was drawing nearer. In his youth Marx had believed that revolutionary action could hasten the changes, but in later life he disdained this idea and in fact appeared impatient with revolutionaries and political activists of all kinds. On the contrary he considered his paradigm of historical stages to be objective, because it was based on a study of material conditions that by their nature produced conflicts which would lead to their destruction and replacement by new conditions. Europe appeared to be moving earliest, because of industrialization and urbanization, toward the stage of socialist transformation, but other parts of the world were still in the early stages of capitalism (for instance, most of North America), while some were feudal (India, China, and the Middle East). Some societies – such as the antebellum South in the United States of America – could combine elements of slave, feudal, and bourgeois stages. But the overriding cultural characteristics of the historical ages were produced, Marx and Engels believed, by the consciousness of each class of its relationship to the sources of wealth and the means of its distribution.

The ideas of Marx and Engels have been adopted and modified all over the world, and applied to the disciplines of history, anthropology, economics, literary criticism, psychology, art history, ecology, medicine and biology, law, women's studies, cultural and ethnic studies, and philosophy. Their application to global history has also been critical, since they propose explanations for universal change that are not diffusionist. Instead, they took ideas about stages of human development that were in some cases thousands of years old and widely occurring in different cultures, made them systematic, and gave them explanations based on the physical and quantifiable conditions of human history. Events were now causes, arising largely from the dynamics of the prevailing and countervailing trends – the contradictions – of major historical stages. To understand contradictions, new research and new evaluations of old research had to be done. And all societies could now be understood in their own terms, not merely as sources or as derivatives as the old diffusionist models would have had it.

The notions of tribal and slave societies were prehistoric, and could be confirmed only by speculation over archeological findings. The socialist and communist futures were purely hypothetical. The real historical problem addressed by Marx and Engels was the transition from feudal to bourgeois society, which had supposedly occurred throughout Europe and North America, as well as in Japan in Marx's own time. If Marx and Engels were correct that feudal societies always preceded capitalist societies, then all currently capitalist societies must have had feudal pasts, and all currently feudal societies should have characteristics indicating how close they are to capitalist transformation. The overwhelming majority of histories, then, should be able to be analyzed on the basis of some future, present, or past relationship to feudalism.

The way was led in the extension of feudalist concepts to histories outside Europe by Russian historians. Even before the revolution of 1917, Pavel N. Miliukov and others wondered whether "feudalism" as conceived by Marx was necessarily a direct development out of a slave period. In some cases, he suggested, it could be the result of pressure by feudalized states upon neighboring societies, which as a result would have to develop the military aristocracy and hierarchical relationships that in Marx's treatment characterized all feudal societies. Miliukov speculated that this explained the slow feudalization in medieval times of both Russia and the Islamic world, which were both pressured by the Byzantine empire. In this way, the introduction of feudalism to societies bordering Europe could be evidence not of universal transformative forces but of a sort of a combination of diffusionism and oppositionalism due to medieval military and economic competition in Eurasia. After the revolution of 1917, historians had even more complex issues in their approach to Marxist historical theory (which, in contrast to the days of Miliukov, was now compulsory). In their view, Russia had led the way toward the history of socialist transformation with its revolution of 1917 and the subsequent policies of Lenin and Stalin to push toward communist transformation of Russia and its attached republics (which in 1922 became the Soviet Union). But if feudalism, capitalism, and socialism were universals of human history, and their dynamics were consistent across the world, the Russian case certainly needed some explanation.

As Miliukov and others had pointed out, early medieval Russia had hardly any aristocracy and no evidence of fiefs. Feudalism had come late to Russia, and stayed a very long time – at least until the emancipation of the serfs in 1861. That left only a blink of the eye for all the contradictions of capitalism to arise, with virtually no industrialization outside a few cities in western Russia, before the Bolshevik revolution of 1917. Fortunately, historians could work with not only the historical materialism of Marx and Engels but also the theoretical interventions of Lenin, who argued (and demonstrated) that certain individuals with revolutionary consciousness could become agents of historical change, hastening and influencing the character of historical transformation. With these enhancements, a Marxist narrative of historical stages could be applied to Russia. Perhaps the most intriguing treatment, and still one of the most influential, came with the publication (in 1934, three years after his death) of Boris Vladimirtsov's study of the origins of Mongol "feudalism." Mainstream Marxist theory denied that nomads could be feudal, as they had no land or agriculture to support a population of serfs or a hierarchy of land grants and military obligations. Yet Vladimirtsov's concept of feudalism followed closely the original arguments of Marx and Engels on the origins of feudalism in the distorted lineage politics of the late slave era. In Vladimirtsov's view, the ancestors of Genghis Khan had used their lineage base to create the rudiments of a feudal state. Genghis, his sons, and grandsons had extended the system throughout Eurasia. The Vladimirtsov thesis was an important part of the puzzle of the USSR, where a significant part of the population were Turkic or Mongol nomads, who in the more conventional view would have to be pushed through not only capitalism but feudalism too. With Vladimirtsov's advancement of nomads along the Marxist timeline, and Lenin's understanding of how the timeline can be shortened, the foundations for a universalist history of Russia were in place.

Japan was an equally important crucible for the development of a universalist Marxist narrative of the transition from feudalism to capitalism. Since Japan's opening to foreign trade in the mid-nineteenth century and its rapid industrialization after the Meiji Restoration of 1868, Europeans and some Americans had been fascinated by the history of the samurai, who were quickly compared to Europe's medieval knights. With the spread of the Marx–Engels interpretation of the importance of the feudal era in understanding the roots of capitalism, the question of whether or not Japan was feudal at the same time as Europe became a topic of early interest. The most definitive approach, and the most famous for several reasons, was that of Asakawa Kan'ichi, born in Japan in 1873 but educated in the United States, where he taught periodically until his death in 1948. In his first study of medieval Japanese legal documents, published in English in 1903 as *The Documents of Iriki*, Asakawa specifically argued that Japan was feudal until the early nineteenth century, when it had showed the characteristics that Marx and Engels had predicted as marking the transition to capitalism. The feudal shogunal state had quickly been destroyed, and then replaced by a constitutional monarchy overseeing industrialization and (it was thought) democratization. Asakawa's painstaking research and clear exposition laid the foundation for a theme in global and comparative history that has continued to flourish. Later studies showed the importance not only of the regional and national leadership of the military aristocracy but also the emergence of nascent capitalism in the provincial market towns and the shogun's capital at Edo (the site of modern Tokyo), the maturing of artisans' skills and an early industrial base, and the rise of a merchant class that could not be contained by the legal and cultural strictures of feudalism. If Japan of all places had not been feudal, the universality of Marx's historical paradigm could not hold, and comparative history as a general issue would be in question.

With Japan firmly in the museum of feudal-to-capitalist transformations, historians of the 1960s and 1970s, in particular, began to add more case studies to the narrative of global feudalism. Chinese historians of the early twentieth century saw the Zhou period of the eleventh to third centuries BCE as being conventionally feudal, with a warrior aristocracy, a social, economic, and political hierarchy based on grants of land and obligations of service. After the communist revolution of 1949, they threw on the two thousand years of imperial history that followed the Zhou; though the empires based in China were centralized and not exclusively based on a warrior aristocracy, the relations between peasants and landlords approximated the relations between serfs and aristocrats, giving a feudal base to China until the early twentieth century. In the 1980s, R. S. Sharma and some other Indian historians argued that India was feudal at roughly the same time as Europe, and especially showed the cultural attributes of deference to feudal elites and local economies that had characterized Europe. But subsequent research into the matters of land grants, government structure, government income, and trade undermined the structural aspects of Sharma's argument. Various parts of the Islamic world, particularly those with a military elite class such as the Mamluk, Seljuk, Ilkhanid, and Ottoman empires, have been argued at various times to be feudal, but legal as well as social studies of feudalism do not match well the characteristics of medieval Islamic societies.

The influence of feudalism as a tool for analysis and narrative of global history has most recently been threatened by two criticisms of the feudalism concept itself. Earliest came the observation, by Marxist-inspired cultural historians, that Marx and Engels were "Eurocentric" in sentiment as well as in historical theory. The supposed universals of historical materialism, the critics argued, were in fact all eccentricities of European development, projected onto foreign histories. The only reason they were regarded as normal, while the patterns of development on other continents were regarded as deviant in one way or another, was because in the lifetimes of Marx and Engels, Europe dominated Asia, Africa, and Latin America, and Europeans thought that their history represented the vanguard of human progress. To the critics, consigning other peoples to "feudal" or "slave" eras was only a new way of excusing European domination. Worse, Marx – generally more acerbic than Engels – had approved of the British invasion of China in the Opium War of 1839. To be fair, Marx at the time was in the clutches of his "oriental mode of production" theory, and thought that China (as well as India and all of Africa) was literally without history – it was stuck in a deviation from the slave society niche that blunted the internal forces of contradiction and transformation. For Marx, China would only begin its history after it came into direct conflict with capitalist and imperialist Britain. In any case, the fashion for finding feudalism in specific places outside Europe was not led by Marx or Engels, but by historians like Charles Beard, Asakawa Kan'ichi, and R. S. Sharma seeking universalist explanations for their local histories. If the experiment failed, it may nevertheless have been a valuable one to pursue.

More serious is the dismantling of feudalism as a tool for the understanding of European history. For many decades the characterization of medieval Europe as "feudal" – by Marxists and non-Marxists alike – had been agreed. But in 1974 Elizabeth A. R. Brown published "The Tyranny of a Construct: Feudalism and Historians of Medieval Europe," arguing that credulous objectification of feudalism by historians was falsely validating phantom explanations for social, economic, and political change in Europe of the late medieval period. Brown's critique was taken up, greatly expanded, and documented by Susan Reynolds in *Fiefs and Vassals* (1994), when she argued that the institutionalization of personal

bonds of vassalage and accompanying land rights that supposedly were general in medieval Europe were actually the
artifacts of a process of legal revision and centralization in
the very late medieval and early modern period, obscuring
important variations in legal development in England, France,
and Italy. For global historians, the question now is what to
do about a concept that has worked well to explain the parallel trajectories of Europe and Japan in the seventeenth through
twentieth centuries, yet now seems to hide more than it
reveals of the specific history from which it was supposed to
be derived.

But the global feudalism model is still survived by its
younger sibling, "modernization." The use of modernization
as a way of understanding universal transformation happening at different places and different times had strong roots in
Marx and Engels, with their understanding of the social and
economic changes required for the transition to capitalism
and the subsequent advance to industrialization. It also
depends greatly upon the ideas of Max Weber, who in the
1880s began his study of the changes in legal and economic
behavior that marked the transition from medieval to early
modern Europe. While some of his contemporaries were
working to elucidate feudalism by contrasting it to capitalism, Weber was working to elucidate capitalism by contrasting it to feudalism. He was unimpressed with Marx's
attribution of all historical change to material forces, and
considered that culture could be a moving force in itself. In
the course of his work he came up with his great complex of
cultural attributes that permitted capitalism and industrialization to flourish uniquely in Europe. In *The Protestant
Ethic and the Spirit of Capitalism* (1904), Weber concluded
that after the Reformation a majority of northern Europeans
cast off the mysticism and unworldliness of the Catholic
Church. Instead, they undertook lives of great personal
discipline, hard work, and personal modesty that caused
them to invest their money in their businesses rather than
spend it on luxuries.

Later economists, sociologists, and cultural historians
would build on Weber's discussion of "rationalization" –
the regularization, professionalization, increased efficiency,
demystification, and openness to experimentation – of

government and society as the universal attributes of "modernization." The economist and political scientist Karl Polanyi used Weberian notions of culturally based economic behavior to explain what he regarded as critical differences between the open and competitive trade patterns of Europe and the defensive, restricted, closed patterns of Asia in the early modern period. His most comprehensive treatment of this approach, which has influenced many anthropologists and sociologists, was *The Great Transformation*, published in 1944. One of the most striking syntheses of Weber and Marx, with a distinct debt to Hegel's original dialecticism, was Thomas Kuhn's *The Structure of Scientific Revolutions* (1962). In it, Kuhn explored the transition points in early modern and modern societies when scientific consensus is forced to confront confirmed anomalies that have not been predicted by the philosophical and ethical assumptions which scientific elites used to define themselves. The necessity of reaching a new synthesis, Kuhn demonstrated, requires the reconstruction of the social and economic frameworks by which science is supported and scientists identified. While he did not regard Europeans as uniformly objective or open in their worldviews, Kuhn did argue that the economic and social changes of early modern Europe created a uniquely productive environment for scientific discovery. The Islamic world, China, and other areas, he implied, were scientifically important mainly for their preservation of ancient knowledge that medieval Europeans lost or rejected. It was their conservatism that distinguished them from innovative, if economically marginal, Europe.

Like industrialization, modernization has become a pillar of contemporary thinking about the large patterns of convergence in the twentieth and twenty-first centuries. Even if Marx and Engels were wrong that all societies must follow a fixed sequence of transformations, many historians, political scientists, and sociologists are convinced that it is a definitive trait of modernization that all cultures will converge. One of the most famous formulations of this hypothesis was the "convergence theory" of Dutch economist Jan Tinbergen, who in several articles of the early 1960s argued that the division of Europe between "capitalist" and "communist" systems would eventually be overcome by the homogenizing effects of living in industrialized societies. The general idea that media access, routinization, time concepts, travel methods, credit cards, and sharing of attitudes about morality that are required by the industrialization process will eventually cause global societies to merge into one society owes a very great debt to Marx and Engels, and to the many historians, sociologists, and economists who have tested and elaborated upon their ideas. The dialog between global historians and Marx's insights will probably never end. Nevertheless, as we will see in the next two chapters there are important dialects of the dialectic, and contradictions over the contradictions, that still keep Marx and Engels at the center of speculation that humanity may be subject to universal material forces that will eventually vanquish all cultural estrangements.

Suggestions for further reading

Asakawa, Kan'ichi, *The Documents of Iriki, Illustrative of the Development of Feudal Institutions of Japan*. (reprint) Westport CT: Greenwood Press, 1974.

Marx, Karl, *Capital: An Abridged Edition*, ed. David McLellan. Oxford: Oxford University Press, 1999.

Morgan, Lewis Henry, *Ancient Society: Or, Researches in the Lines of Human Progress from Savagery through Barbarism to Civilization*. Boston MA: Adamant Media Corporation, 2004.

Reynolds, Susan, *Fiefs and Vassals: The Medieval Evidence Reinterpreted*. New York: Oxford University Press, 1996.

Watson, Andrew M., *Agricultural Innovation in the Early Islamic World: The Diffusion of Crops and Farming Techniques, 700–1100*. Cambridge: Cambridge University Press, 1983.

4
Contagion

In the previous two chapters we examined ways in which universal or global historians used concepts of change to explain very large transitions in human economic, technological, and cultural life. Contact between very different communities was an important dynamic in both the divergent and the convergent models. In the case of diffusion or divergence, contact was a way of transmitting information, cultural influences, or – in the most modern models – genes between communities that had already diversified from an original homogeneous condition. In the case of convergence, contact could be a factor in accelerating structural change that was not dependent on other similarities between societies, or could be a partial explanation for delayed transformation. Yet there are also models of human history that take contact, or contagion, as the most fundamental explanation for change. In this understanding, influences that have been introduced by contact with a distinctly different community – whether language, religion, technology, artistic styles, or disease – take on a new life in the receiving community. They may become more important, or more destabilizing, in the new environment than they were in the old. Many very important global historians have taken the idea of contagion, infestation, or epidemic as both a literal issue and a figurative description of a self-propelling element of change, usually moving rapidly and having an effect of some magnitude.

Historians in 1960 read the bacteriologist Hans Zinsser's *Rats, Lice and History*, which demonstrated that at some critical points infectious disease had tilted the fortunes of war and diplomacy. In general, Zinsser's characterization of the role of plagues appeared to be analogous to the functions of earthquakes, volcanic eruptions, and asteroid strikes, as severe but serendipitous events that could momentarily negate the attempts of humans to control their own fates. In that respect, disease had long been appreciated as a decisive force. The ancient historian Thucydides had considered plague a factor in the outcome of the Peleponnesian Wars, and Procopius had described a famous plague of the 500s CE that had afflicted Constantinople. In China, the fourth-century CE Daoist Ge Hong had described an epidemic that closely resembled bubonic plague which disrupted north China in a period of disunion. Historians had long recognized the impact in fourteenth-century Europe of the Black Death, when a third of the population was concluded to have died, and the damage to urban centers and professional elites had been profound enough to have far-reaching economic, social, and ultimately cultural effects. Edward Gibbon's *Decline and Fall of the Roman Empire*, particularly in its discussion of the Byzantine empire and of the Crusades, repeatedly introduced disease as an explanation for the success of "barbarian" troops against Christians. Zinsser's book was scientifically authoritative and intriguing to read, and historians began to cite it frequently, but it was not conceptually new to historians.

The seminal study that transformed understanding of the role of disease from a simple diffusion model to one of contagion was Alfred Crosby's *The Columbian Exchange: Biological and Cultural Consequences of 1492*, in 1972. Crosby argued that while small numbers of people had often traveled across and between continents in the past, effecting some degree of genetic and microbial exchange among distant populations, the very late 1400s marked a threshold of revolutionary increase in new physical contact between Europeans and Africans, Americans, and the peoples of some Atlantic islands. It was not only the peoples themselves who traveled. They brought their horses and cattle, seeds for their crops, and their clothing, in which disease-carrying insects of Europe

could conceal themselves. The results for many of the populations with whom they came in contact, Crosby pointed out,
were devastating. The ancestors of the peoples of America
had come from extreme Northeast Asia and then lived isolated from Eurasia for perhaps 10,000 years. Unlike Asians
of the 1400s, Americans had never been exposed to smallpox
or to bubonic plague. Their populations, even though in
some areas relatively dense due to developed agriculture,
never reached the urban concentrations of a million or more
necessary to experience and develop immunity to the most
virulent airborne diseases such as tuberculosis or whooping
cough. Upon contact with bubonic plague and subsequently
with smallpox, measles, cholera, and other infections, peoples
of the Caribbean and of the American mainland died in
huge numbers. They were able to offer little resistance to
even small-scale military invasion by Europeans, and their
numbers were insufficient to maintain the influence of
their cultures.

Nevertheless, Crosby argued, while the exchange was lop-
sided it was truly an exchange. For their part, Europeans had
not previously had syphilis. Once they contracted it from the
peoples of the Americas, it spread rapidly through Europe
and permanently changed many aspects of European life.
Crosby noted that the first outbreak of syphilis in Europe – in
Naples, Italy in 1494 – may well have been due to the return
of Columbus's crew. The effects could not mirror the effects
at the other end of the exchange, primarily because syphilis
can be slow in developing; because it is related to infectious
agents that had a long history in Europe such as tuberculosis,
Europeans were quick to develop a partial immunity. Within
roughly a century the disease was contained in Europe, with
a persisting low rate of infection and complication. In a later
book, *Ecological Imperialism: The Biological Expansion of
Europe, 900–1900* (1986), Crosby attributed Europeans'
relative resistance to infectious diseases to differences in their
imperialist behaviors. In Africa, the Middle East, and India,
Crosby found, Europeans were more susceptible to local
disease and the local people more resistant to European infections. As a result, in those areas European imperialism took
the form of superficial and predatory administrations imposed
upon but segregated from the majority local population. In

the Americas, Australia, and islands of the Atlantic, the epidemiological advantages of the Europeans led to wholesale displacement of the local populations, with ensuing environmental changes reinforcing the European advantages.

In 1990, Crosby's study of the influenza pandemic of 1918, *America's Forgotten Pandemic: The Influenza of 1918*, suggested the shift of disease generation and dissemination from Europe to America. By the time of World War I, global conditions of transportation and colonialism were such that only a small island at the mouth of the Amazon could avoid infection altogether, and only a few Pacific islands managed to avoid deaths from the epidemic that originated in Kansas. By the end of the epidemic in 1919, it is possible that worldwide a hundred million people had died of the disease, perhaps ten times as many as were killed in World War I. The greatest proportions of deaths to total population were in the United States, with the most intense local fatality rate in Alaska. Pacific islands also had very high proportional losses, as did China and India. The smallest proportional losses among developed nations were in Britain and Japan. The assumption of present-day researchers is that for many reasons – including the basic virology of the pandemic as well as modern patterns of transmission and management – the relationship of the history of the 1918 pandemic to basic mechanisms of global development predict the progress of present and future highly contagious diseases, particularly the group of viruses thought to cause avian flu.

In 1976, a Canadian-born historian at the University of Chicago, William H. McNeill, published his *Plagues and Peoples*. McNeill expanded the contagion model to encompass many aspects of transformation following new exchanges between remote cultures. According to his much-quoted introduction to the book, he first became interested in the role of disease in history when reading accounts of the Spanish invasion of the Aztec empire, which with millions of subjects and a substantial army apparently could not resist the few hundred conquistadors under Hernando Cortes. This amazing phenomenon had been conventionally explained as the Aztecs being somehow in awe of the Europeans, seemingly on sight. Indeed, the Aztecs were reported by earlier historians to have regarded the Europeans as gods, or as agents of the "white" god Quetzlcoatl, and their horses as all-powerful magical beasts. McNeill was skeptical. Even if these apprehensions had seized the Aztecs momentarily, how could they have survived any actual battle, in which horses and Europeans would be wounded and killed like anybody else? The Europeans had guns, but not unlimited ammunition. Any unified resistance by the Aztecs would eventually have overwhelmed the invading force. Even more puzzling to McNeill was the explosive dominance of Spanish culture, including Roman Catholicism, in the Americas so soon after the arrival of Europeans. The Aztecs were only the last of a series of empires in Central America with large populations, highly developed agriculture, stable governments, established religious traditions with complex hierarchies, and proven military competence. How could these great traditions have withered so rapidly, especially when the colonial government was so small and rudimentary?

McNeill suspected that the explanation was more than incidental and related to something that rapidly and profoundly diminished both the effectiveness of Aztec resistance and the numbers of the Aztecs themselves. Contemporary accounts from the time suggested to him that the Aztecs had become ill, massively and suddenly, from something the Spanish identified as smallpox, and that this illness affected the Aztecs after they had successfully repelled the Spanish forces from the Aztec capital of Tenochtitlan. McNeill surmised that the Spanish, who would have been resistant to smallpox, had unwittingly infected the Aztecs. The disease spread among the Aztecs with extraordinary ferocity. If the Aztecs had indeed experienced any awe of Europeans and their religion, McNeill suggested, it was more likely to have arisen from the apparent Spanish invulnerability to the blight, while Aztecs sickened, suffered, and died. He found similar explanations for the fall of the Inca empire, and for the weak resistance of natives of North America to incursions by the Spanish, French, and English. On examining the dynamics of disease in the regions of the world with very densely populated cities and heavily used trade routes in North Africa, Eurasia, and the Indian Ocean, McNeill emphasized the phenomenon of the "pandemic" – intertwining epidemics in which a primary infection, usually bubonic plague or smallpox, weakens the general resistance of affected populations which then succumb to secondary infections such as pneumonia. As in the case of simple epidemics, the dynamics of self-limitation – mass death of the susceptible, combined with recovery and reproduction of the resistant – brought an end to each pandemic, causing the primary disease to retreat and evolve until it had opportunity to strike again. The explanation for the explosion and dissipation of epidemic disease was the mutually interacting regional histories of human resistance. Where Crosby saw the sea-crossing of large numbers of Europeans to the Americas as the critical event in human history, McNeill saw it in the transition to farming and animal domestication. Those developments, he argued, had brought humans into new, close, sustained contact with animals who had their own range of infectious diseases, but also allowed humans to live in dense population groups (particularly across Eurasia) where infection, resistance, and mutation cycles were dramatically speeded up.

McNeill's discussion of infectious illness in this work was so influential that for more than a decade disease as a result of new cross-cultural contacts, and its far-reaching effects on systems of trade, settlement, government, and defense, became the focus of activity for historians seeking a global or world perspective. *Yersinia pestis*, the bacillus that caused bubonic plague, became one of the most famous figures in history. Students of all ages began to learn of *Y. pestis'* ability to multiply in the guts of – and eventually to starve – fleas, who in turn ride on the backs of steppe-crossing marmots and sea-faring rats, looking for larger, bloodier, and warmer hosts to satisfy their increasing hunger. Eventually the dying but insatiable fleas find and bite humans, who then develop the disease that progresses to an airborne state that envelops and kills those nearby.

Some historians questioned McNeill's identification of epidemics before the Black Death in Europe as bubonic plague rather than typhus or smallpox, and by extension whether earlier exposure would have accounted for the survival of most Europeans during the Black Death. But for those developing epidemiology as a larger field of historical research, other diseases soon got some attention, too. Crosby's theory of the Columbian exchange was challenged by evidence from medieval European burials, in which some remains seemed to show evidence of syphilis before Columbus's voyages. Crosby responded that the evidence could as easily indicate a variant of tuberculosis, whose long history in Europe Crosby had already credited with Europe's quick adaptation to the introduction of syphilis. The two diseases, Crosby argued, are closely related, with syphilis a variant of tuberculosis that developed uniquely in the Americas before the arrival of Columbus. At this date, the syphilis issue is still unresolved. Such disagreements have inspired historians and biologists and geneticists to undertake studies of the natural histories of major diseases. As a consequence we know that some diseases, such as rickets and tuberculosis, are as old as the human species. Others, such as smallpox, measles, and the common cold, are part of the history of animal domestication. And others, such as environmental cancers and AIDS, are modern. The longevity and the virulence of a disease's association with humanity leaves its mark both upon the disease itself and upon human evolution.

The development of global historical conceptions was more profoundly influenced by the expanded contagion analysis in McNeill's work. His initial interest was not only in the material effects of illness upon the Aztecs, but also the parallel effects upon Aztec culture. He called this fundamental analytical device in the book "parasitism." In the relationship with its host, the parasite seeks opportunities to thrive through exploitation, either of a living host, or of a new host if the old one should be unable to survive. A parasite linked to a single host with no hope of relocating must tie its future to the future of its host, and adapt its behavior to allow the host to survive. For McNeill, the model was biological, ecological, economic, social, and political. The effects upon the human body of the biological mechanisms of disease, resistance, immunity and evolution was what McNeill regarded as "microparasitism." Host and parasite relations between humans and other animals, between human individuals, communities, states, and empires he regarded as types of "macroparasitism." McNeill suggested in *Plagues and Peoples* that what were normally described as "opportunistic infections," or the exploitation by bacteria or viruses of weaknesses in the human immune system, could also be not only literal microparasitic phenomena but also models of macroparasitic interaction, explaining slavery and feudalism (two problems that were famous for their theoretical explanation by Marx and Engels), as well as crime, civil wars, revolutions, foreign invasions, and imperialism.

In a later work, *The Global Condition: Conquerors, Catastrophes and Communities* (1992), McNeill returned to and developed his large theory of macroparasitism. In it, McNeill was able to sketch out the arc of his model, which clearly contrasted to convergence models before it. Unlike Marx and those deriving their historical concepts from his, McNeill's understanding of macroparasitism predicted no culmination of history. The dynamics of exploitation and survival in the model mandated an exchange in which parasite and host must both receive benefits from their symbiosis. So long as those conditions pertain, the cycles of infection, adaptation, and exchange could continue indefinitely. But a pathological parasitism in which the benefits to the host have fallen too low or disappeared will result in the death of the host. Unless the parasite finds a new host, the parasite will expire as well. The only end to the cycle of macroparasitic symbiosis would be the exhaustion of the resources necessary to support all hosts. That extreme end, McNeill suggested, could be delayed by everything that strengthened human solidarity, or human resistance to parasitical exploitation: technologies, language, love, families, communities of various sizes and functions, and governments. But maladaptation, including the unwise or inappropriate application of technology, could hasten resource exhaustion. *The Global Condition* added little to McNeill's earlier insights in *Plagues and Peoples*, and in some cases may have stretched the model to its breaking point. However, it not only reminded historians of the potential of the contagion model as an explanation of global change, but also directed their attention to the most literally fundamental resources of human hosts and parasites: the natural environment. Not surprisingly, later work by McNeill and his son John R. McNeill elaborated upon the importance of the history of the natural environment in understanding universal human conditions.

Both Crosby and McNeill had emphasized that genetic diffusion and environmental change were unavoidable aspects of trade and imperialism. Long-distance trade was motivated by a supply-and-demand dynamic that resembled opportunistic infection at its inception and in the case of well-developed market centers assumed a macroparasitic relation to its host. As empires sent out their explorers, administrators, and colonists, they also sent out their bacilli and viruses, and – as Cavalli-Sforza's "dual inheritance" theory had proposed – their genes. But McNeill had suggested that imperialism itself was an opportunistic infection, exploiting loopholes just as infectious agents would do. Sparse population and lack of urban centers, agricultural development, or strong political organizations were all fundamental attractors of invasion yet did not assure the success or permanence of imperialist exploitation. In many cases areas of great microparasitic complexity and resistance – such as India and China – could demonstrate significant weakness in the macroparasitic context, leaving them open to more aggressive, more industrialized, more militarily efficient predators. Once established, imperialists assumed the same parasitic relationship to their colonized host that commercial suppliers assumed with respect to their consumers. A successfully symbiotic relationship would endure; a pathologically parasitical relationship would be quickly dissolved through war or revolution.

In 1997, Sheldon Watts's *Epidemics and History: Disease, Power and Imperialism* took up the theme of global vulnerabilities and responses to disease to argue that disease was not merely an unavoidable element of imperialism, but was indispensable both to the process of imperialism and to our understanding of what imperialism is. Watts pointed out that the dynamics of immunity cast some doubt upon the persuasiveness of McNeill's thesis alone. While it was certainly true that some populations enjoyed significant immunity and that the larger and denser the population the more immune factors would be present in the population as a whole, individual humans are born without much immunity and must acquire it, no matter who they are or where they live. That being the case, Watts considered it unlikely that Europeans encountering new populations in the course of imperialist incursions were really as uniformly resistant to disease as McNeill had suggested. Medieval European success in surviving the epidemics and then surviving diseases they transmitted to newly encountered populations in the early modern period could not be attributable to long-term, stable, quasi-racial attributes of Europeans; therefore that success must have cultural, social, or political explanations. Watts drew upon the insights of Crosby regarding ecologically strategic imperialist patterns, as well as the ideas of cultural historians interested in alterity – explanations related to concepts of the "other" – to look at how Europeans handled diseases differently from the peoples with whom they developed imperialist connections. He suggested that the age of imperialist expansion for European nations (particularly Britain) coincided with a new stage in the construction of cultural ideas about the alienness of Asians, Africans, and the peoples of the Americas. An early form of this construction was medieval European anti-Semitism, which prescribed separate communities – ghettoes – for Jews. When the Black Death arrived, the European cities quickly responded with quarantine, an idea they were familiar with because of the ghetto tradition. This helped limit the infection, augmenting the naturally self-limiting workings of the epidemic.

This approach contrasted with that of Egypt under the Mamluk sultans. Trade between Kaffa on the Black Sea – where plague was first noted in the fourteenth century – and Cairo created a cycle of epidemic and dormancy at both ends of the route. The Mamluks refused to use quarantine to limit spread of the illness, since they (unlike some other areas of the Islamic world) did not observe any tax or legal differences between Jews and others, and had no concept of systematically, physically isolating some segments of the population. In the case of plague and smallpox, the culturally peculiar practice of quarantine aided Europeans in avoiding or surviving infection, but in other cases Watts noted that Europeans practiced forms of quarantine or abstinence even when there was no good reason for it. Leprosy, for instance, is not highly contagious and in most societies outside Europe was not regarded with horror; only Europeans were so undone at the idea of leprosy that they created virtually leper-only zones in various parts of the world, most famously on Molokai Island near Hawaii. In the same way, Europeans responded to their acquisition of syphilis (which Watts seems to agree came after their contact with the Americas) with such panic that they divided society between the "pure," or sexually disciplined – those who ostensibly did not masturbate, have sexual affairs outside marriage, or engage in homosexuality – and the "impure," or sexually undisciplined (masturbators, adulterers, and prostitutes of both sexes). The paradoxical result was an epidemic of syphilis, as all sexual behaviors not regarded as pure were consigned to the realms of ignorance, secrecy, and hypocrisy. Most insidious, Europeans could not see themselves as the originators of disease, instead seeing themselves always vulnerable to pollution by aliens and alien diseases. In colonial venues in which the European behavior was in fact the source of the disease or cause of its spread – most dramatically in the Indian cholera epidemics of the 1850s – British colonial authorities never looked to themselves to understand the dynamics of the disease, instead determinedly building new vectors of infection by extending canals and open water sources in order to improve the local "hygiene." This, Watts points out, was a dramatic contrast to London, where wells were quickly identified as the source of infection and capped or treated.

Reviewers of Watts's book noted that the idea of "social construction" of knowledge was not always well applied to medicine. Analysis of some forms of knowledge as primarily social constructions might make sense, they pointed out, when many facts are available and some are chosen over others merely because they conform to the underlying assumptions that societies are projecting as "knowledge." But when a society truly has very little knowledge – in the way that Europeans had comparatively little knowledge of medicine or hygiene before the nineteenth century – the influence of social construction may be so weak as to be insignificant. In the sixteenth and seventeenth centuries, the Chinese and some parts of the Islamic world understood variolation, and were able to effect a certain amount of immunity in themselves with this technology. These areas of the world were also comparatively advanced in knowledge of pharmacology. Through their experiences in trade and role as imperialists Europeans learned some of these sciences rather late, and in the meantime made do with folk assumptions and even racial theories. As for the British and cholera in India, cholera had in fact spread from India to London in the early nineteenth century, and it was not completely a construction to think that India was in some way profoundly and persistently affected by cholera. The Indians, of course, had known for millennia of effective ways to purify water, and knew that the measures imposed by the British were only spreading the disease further. The history of modern British epidemiology is largely the history of British researchers discovering how to manage infectious diseases encountered only in colonial contexts where Indians, Chinese, or Africans had lived successfully (through their own management of infectious disease) for millennia. Nevertheless, scholarship such as Watts's was a valuable extension of work on cultural history that reads conceptualization of the body and disease as projections of society's understanding of power, racial superiority, and sexual oppression. Discursive studies of empire and the construction of race, gender, beauty, morality, and health are rich, and stand – like Watts's book – in strong contrast to the more materialist approaches taken by earlier scholars of epidemiology, ecology, and technology under imperialism.

In the same year that Watts' book was published, the biologist Jared Diamond published his hyper-materialist tome, *Guns, Germs and Steel: The Fates of Human Societies* (whose title echoed Crosby's 1994 *Germs, Seeds and Animals*). In it, the paths explored by Crosby and developed by McNeill were widened. The effects of the transition to agriculture on human population and disease history, the role of domestic animals in enriching the human immunity palette, and the advantages of Eurasia as a large, complex, widely diversified matrix of genetic and technological exchange were already ideas well entrenched in the discourse of global history. Diamond added a dimension of geography, explaining that the relative isolation of Africa and the Americas in contrast to Eurasia resulted in paucity of population and challenges to immunity, which left them unprepared in many ways for the onslaught of industrialized, disease-resistant Europeans in the early modern and modern periods. The primary difference between Diamond's explanations for large historical changes and those already well known to students of global history was that he gave geography and environment decisive weight over other factors such as culture, trade, and even technology (which he regarded as primarily derived from the interaction of environment and demography). Diamond's book was influential in inspiring greater public interest in global history. Many historians, however, were puzzled by both the claims of the book to originality and its terse conclusions about the power configurations of the world in the modern period. In his introduction, Diamond argued that he was choosing to emphasize the role of environmental factors in history in order to combat a dominant racism and culturalism in most historical writing; his purpose, he explained, was to defend cultures outside Europe as being equal to European culture, and peoples outside Europe as being as "intelligent" as Europeans. But by the time Diamond was writing, such assumptions had been long rejected by most historians, and sectors of the profession were ever-vigilant in seeking out and criticizing writing that seemed evocative of them.

William McNeill himself appreciated Diamond's confirmation of the basic science behind explanations such as his regarding the role of germs and resistance in human history, but derided as "absurd" Diamond's assertion of primary environmental determination, arguing that throughout their history humans had been transforming the environment, for motivations cultural, economic, and social. Other historians, and the geographer J. M. Blaut, pointed out that the historical evidence was in many cases thin, distorted, or absent in supporting Diamond's arguments. One of the more interesting observations in Diamond's book was that the Americas and Australia were alike not only in the sparsity and isolation of their human populations in early times, but also in the ways in which their very large animals of the period at the end of the last Ice Age had been completely displaced by newly arrived humans. He suggested that animal populations who had gone to these isolated regions before humans arrived had experienced genetic specialization, immunological isolation, and lack of challenges that would have required rapid adaptation. As a consequence, these large animals – megafauna – had been easily exterminated, which according to Diamond reduced opportunities for animal domestication in Australia and the Americas. It is not clear that megafauna, by any definition, have been the main source of domesticated animals. But historians were more puzzled by the fact that Diamond's explanations did not address a dramatic difference between the Americas and Australia: The peoples of the Americas had been among the earliest and most successful at agriculture, and had domesticated many animals, including llama and cavies (guinea pigs), and been receptive to the husbandry of imported animals (such as chickens, brought to the Americas by Pacific Islanders some hundreds of years before Columbus). In Australia, however, the native population never developed agriculture, despite having a temperate climate comparable to the northern hemisphere. The mystery is deepened by the fact that the early inhabitants of Papua New Guinea, not far from Australia (and the site of much of Diamond's scientific research in earlier times), were possibly among the earliest agriculturalists in the world. Diamond's explanation – that Australians had never had the opportunity to come into contact with agriculture – struck many historians as an unconvincing throwback to the diffusionist ideas of late nineteenth-century Europe.

A similar problem occurred in relation to the loss of agriculture among the Bantu speakers after their migration from Central Africa to what is now South Africa. They were agriculturalists before the move, and not after. Diamond's explanation was that their former crops were unsuitable, and that the new environment had no plants suitable for domestication. But in fact, the Xhosa people of the area were already practicing agriculture. Why would the new arrivals not adapt the crop? Geneticists, anthropologists, and others noted that because of the long history of human habitation in Africa, its populations were the most genetically diverse and probably the most immune. Why would they not, according to Diamond's theory, have emerged as the most populous, most urban, and most technologically advanced? Diamond's implied explanation was that in Africa, as in the Americas, migrations due to population growth were forced into a north–south channel, unlike the east–west channels made possible by the geography of Eurasia. This caused peoples, like the Bantu-speakers, to transfer to climatically unfamiliar environments; instead of building on existing skills in farming and health management, they were required constantly to reinvent their cultures and sciences to adapt. However, this hardly explained the fact that current theories of early population development in the Americas propose overwhelmingly north and south migration, yet these continents – including the very nexus of this migration, Central America – were in fact among the world's most agriculturally developed, most populous, and possibly even most scientifically advanced societies of medieval times. What happened? In the instances of Central America and the Middle East, Diamond suggested that the populations had outstripped the ability of the environmental resources to support them. There is certainly evidence for this. But the intrusion of marginal, haphazard, or anomalous events in Diamond's explanations made some readers skeptical that environmental determinism could explain everything.

Most historians found Diamond's arguments that Eurasia had a specific advantage because most people lived there helpful for explaining to undergraduates that Europe and China were not culturally or racially "superior" to other regions; beyond that, the book's theory of causations had problems with tautology and superficiality. Few had to be convinced that where there were many people in continuous communication there were many ideas and many opportunities to test them. Where many different societies come into contact there will be many opportunities to encounter pathogens and develop immunity. Where there are many different technologies there will be many opportunities to compare and develop them. But the specific dynamics of Diamond's argument required certain historical developments, not all of which happened. For instance, according to Diamond the reason for the early and continuing prominence of China was the fact that China's geography was suitable for agriculture, it had an extensive central plain that allowed an orderly and continuously centralized expansion of population, and it had no natural obstacles to constant contact with the Silk Roads connecting it to Central Asia, South Asia, the Middle East, and ultimately Europe. With these optimal conditions, China should have been the earliest society throughout eastern Eurasia to develop all technologies and its political dominance should have been continuous. In some ways, the role Diamond theoretically prescribed for China resembled that which Joseph Needham had asserted (see chapter 2). Yet, modern research revealed that, like its neighboring (and less environmentally blessed) Asian societies, China had been both an originator and a recipient of technologies. It was not continuously unified but had spent nearly half its history disunified and often under the partial or entire political domination of foreign invaders. Unlike the instances of Australia and southern Africa, Diamond offered no explanation for why, in the nineteenth and early twentieth centuries, China had in fact become one of the poorer and weaker societies in the world; he simply suspended his discussion of Chinese history after the late Ming period, roughly the sixteenth century, at which time China was still in the ranks of world leaders for economy, technology, wealth, and population.

J. M. Blaut, who singled out Diamond as one of the "Eight Most Eurocentric Historians," concluded that Diamond's arguments were not only unconvincing on their own terms but at bottom shared the assumptions of European importance and normality that Diamond claimed to reject. While Diamond's emphasis on Eurasia as a single geographical and historical entity was significant and harmonious with many currents in contemporary historical research and narrative, Blaut insisted that it was only a way of obscuring the fact that Diamond was actually concerned primarily with Europe and its global domination in nineteenth and twentieth centuries as the central issue of history itself. For all his efforts to break free of the weight of the question of how and why Europe and then the United States so dominated the world in the nineteenth and twentieth centuries, Blaut claimed that Diamond had only ended up making the same assumptions and asking the same questions as those he had intended to refute. As we will see in the next two chapters, it was this criticism, above all others, that makes Diamond's work a point of interest for those of us wondering exactly what, in the end, global history is.

Suggestions for further reading

Crosby, Alfred, *Ecological Imperialism: The Biological Expansion of Europe, 900–1900*. Cambridge: Cambridge University Press, 1986.

Diamond, Jared, *Guns, Germs and Steel: The Fates of Human Societies*. New York: W. W. Norton, 1997.

Marks, Robert B., *The Origins of the Modern World: A Global and Ecological Narrative from the Fifteenth to the Twenty-first Cenutry*. Lanham MD: Rowman & Littlefield, 2006.

McNeill, William H., *Plagues and Peoples*. Garden City NJ: Doubleday/Anchor, 1976.

Watts, Sheldon, *Epidemics and History: Disease, Power and Imperialism*. New Haven CT: Yale University Press, 1997.

5
Systems

The perspective of global historians must be wide in both space and time, the better to understand the working of large patterns in human history. Diffusionist approaches had understood time and space as being related to a distant point of origin for history and human culture; over millennia, early similarities and proximity had become differences and distance. Theorists of dialectical change, on the other hand, saw the effects of time as imposing transformational processes on distinct societies that would cause differences, no matter how widely spaced, to eventually become fundamental similarities. Some of the most recent influential global historians, however, have tended to think and narrate in terms of systems – distinct parts that work together in a coherent way, tending toward stability unless a destructive (perhaps intrusive) factor causes the system to disintegrate or collapse.

A few cultures had a history of systemic thinking about culture and history before the nineteenth century. In China, for instance, the philosopher Xunzi during the third century BCE thought that early human history was governed by a principle of "grouping" (*qun*), which accounted for people wanting to live in communities and cooperate with each other, rather than live solitary or completely competitive lives. In the seventeenth century some Chinese philosophers picked up the idea and gave it a racial aspect: They argued that grouping was a cosmological principle that explained how the universe evolved from an original homogeneous state into the world of material differences known in their time. These material differences, they thought, were expressed in human racial differences the same as they were in the differences between water and rock. People of the same kind would be attracted to each other and repelled by people who were different. In this way, they claimed not only to understand the differences between Chinese and Mongols, or Chinese and Manchus, but also to be able to explain why it was fundamentally immoral for one people to forcibly conquer and rule another. In the early twentieth century, Chinese thinkers modernized grouping as nationalism.

Other cultures also had some comparable ideas about the dynamics causing communities to cohere and to compete against each other. Abu Zaid Abdurrahman ibn Muhammad ibn Khaldun al-Hadrami, the fourteenth-century historian of North Africa and particularly of the Berbers, was famous for his formalization of historical inquiry, writing out a method of approaching documents skeptically. Ibn Khaldun rejected the idea that history is local or national, and prefaced his detailed treatment of Berber history and society with a "world history" in the style of Rashid al-Din (see chapter 1). He also suggested systems dynamics in history, particularly between nomads and urban populations. The most powerful determinant of changing political and social configurations, for Ibn Khaldun, was "solidarity" (*asabiyya*). This was the accumulation of material factors, including ancestry and blood relationships, that provided the momentum for community formation and survival, as well as the resources to overcome militarily the obstacles dividing the religious world of Islam. These ideas, as it happens, are both relevant to some theories of global history that we will take up in the next chapter of this book.

Modern systems theory, however, is normally associated with Europe and North America, and its most direct roots can be traced to the generalized influence of Charles Darwin and Karl Marx. Like most of their systems-oriented descendants, Darwin and Marx both attributed change to material factors, exclusively. They both proposed that change was a result of the internal workings of the system as they understood it. For Darwin, the interaction of the natural environment and genetic adaptation of some sort (in Darwin's time the working of genes was not well understood) produced a "natural selection" effect, and the dynamics of that system were adequate to explain the large patterns of change. For Marx, the conflicts between many complex factors, but fundamentally the aspirations of the majority for security and independence and the determination of a minority to dominate the proceeds of the general labor, produced trends that transform present relationships between work and reward, and create new relationships between them that will also be destroyed in the future. In both cases, the system was understood to be self-generating. For Darwin, it was also self-correcting. For Marx, it was self-transforming.

As we noted in the previous chapter, Marx was criticized in his own time, and much more in later times, for being primarily focused on Europe. In his early career he thought that societies of Africa and Asia literally had no history, since they appeared to have fallen off the road of transforming contradictions and stresses that caused historical change. At best, he once thought, they were subject to fluctuations in productivity and to dynastic changes of government. Later, Marx modified this view, but still assumed that the stages and the pace of European history were the pattern of normal historical change. Regions that were still slave, or still feudal, or combined them in some way, were deviations that historians must explain as exposing some weakness in the ways that transformation had been suppressed or expressed in those regions. At the same time, in its relations with other continents, Marx certainly saw Europe as the leading and determinative actor. Africa, Asia, and the Americas were subject to European exploitation, and their own development came primarily from their reaction against imperialism, which was itself an attempt by Europe to compensate for the contradictions of capitalism. These two characteristics of Marx's thought have remained, until recently, outstanding characteristics of historical systems theories. However, one very brilliant historian offered an early challenge.

The Belgian historian Henri Pirenne was well established as an authority on the medieval history of his country when the Germans invaded it in 1914. For a few years Pirenne peacefully protested the German occupation, but in 1916 the

Germans lost patience with him and put him in a prison camp. There, deprived of the ability to find out more facts, he began to think in terms of interpretations. The idea he emerged with, and soon after the war made the basis of lectures and a series of books, was what we now call the "Pirenne thesis." Contrary to the consensus among historians of Europe that the fall of the Roman empire had marked the line between classical times and the "Middle Ages," Pirenne argued that Roman culture, law, and identities had persisted for centuries. Economic and cultural development could have continued in Europe through the medieval period except for one great event: the conquest of Spain and Portugal, as well as disruption of sea access, by the new Islamic empire under the Umayyad dynasty. Because of that, Pirenne concluded, Europe's economic contacts with the rest of Eurasia were disrupted, causing the European economy to shrivel, inhibiting its technological development, and only at length producing the economic and cultural decline normally associated with the "Dark Ages." At the same time, Eastern Europe – where the Byzantine empire continued much of the government, culture, and economics of the Roman empire – became distinct from isolated Western Europe.

Pirenne's evidence for the consequence of western European isolation was all material. Trade goods that had been familiar to Europeans in Roman times such as spices, perfumes, wine, and olive oil, became rare and expensive. Gold coins were displaced by cheaper silver, and some areas gave up minting coins at all, suggesting that their economies had devolved toward barter. The merchant class largely disappeared, with only remnants remaining in some Jewish quarters of some cities. Christian access to seaways continued only in areas such as the eastern Mediterranean where some merchants had engaged in cooperative relationships with Muslim sponsors. These conditions, Pirenne argued, were all the fundamental factors behind the emergence of the new Holy Roman Empire under Charlemagne and his campaigns. The period of Charlemagne, as Pirenne saw it, was revolutionary and not a continuation of the petty Western European kingdoms that preceded it. The pope was now allied with Western Europe, and not vaguely associated with both Byzantium and Charlemagne personally. A new Western European mission was defined in Charlemagne's successful wars to stop further Islamic conquests in Europe. His regime, built upon the war governments of his direct ancestors, was more centralized, and definitively based upon the privileges and the responsibilities of the military class. It was the amalgam of militarism, centrality, and religious legitimacy under Charlemagne that in Pirenne's interpretation was the foundation for late medieval Europe. And none of that, he argued, would have happened without the Islamic incursions and occupation.

Much in Pirenne's thesis explained more about local history than global history, and it is perhaps not surprising that it had more than a little in common with the "Mongol yoke" theory of Russian history (already partially developed in the mid-1800s by Alexander Pushkin), in which the Mongols play the role of the Muslims and disrupt Russian progress out of feudalism by isolating Russia from Byzantium and from Western Europe. And much of the detail in Pirenne's thesis was later criticized by historians who found evidence that the minting of coins had continued at a higher rate than Pirenne had supposed, or that changes in land control did not conform well to Pirenne's ideas of when power in Europe had shifted to the military class; other details associated with Pirenne's characterization of early medieval Europe's depressed economy were apparently overstated. What is important to note is that at bottom Pirenne's thesis had three iconoclastic elements. First, it transcended conventional periodization, linking deep changes not to superficial political crises such as the fall of Rome but to more long-term, fundamental structural issues of trade. Second, it posited a transformative, dynamic relationship between two very different parts of the world that had previously been narrated by historians as independent of each other. Third, it placed the impetus of European change outside of Europe, an inversion of the historical geography that Marx had outlined and that most European historians found incontrovertible. Not surprisingly, Pirenne's son Jacques, inspired by his father's ideas, would in 1948 contribute the harbinger of modern world history texts, *Les grands courants de l'histoire universelle* (later translated as *The Tides of History*).

In 1953, the Swedish historian Sture Bolin suggested that actual geo-economic relationships had been reversed in the

Pirenne thesis. Rather than being economically inhibited by the Islamic occupation of Spain and Portugal, parts of the European economy had actually been stimulated because of peripheral contact with the rich trade networks of the Muslim world. Bolin's research indicated that Western Europe in particular had been a supplier of natural resources (including human slaves) to the Islamic economy in exchange for luxury goods and cash. Complex sub-networks in the trade had encompassed Russia and reached to Scandinavia (a fact we touched in chapter 1 in reference to Ibn Fadlan). Though Bolin's description of an exuberant Western European economy responding to the stimulus of the Islamic trade networks was criticized by some historians for its details and eventually qualified, in the long run it was his building on the basic features of Pirenne that shaped an emerging view of historical dynamics. Pirenne's vision, especially as qualified by Bolin, was of a system: the Islamic empire's economy and the local economies of Europe interacted in such as way as to transform Europe itself, which in turn initiated a series of changes that contributed to the later destruction of the Islamic empire. In this case, the Islamic trade system was the originating actor, and Europe the reactive one. The basic schema as outlined by Bolin later reappeared in Janet Abu-Lughod's *Before European Hegemony* (1989), which argued that the generation of wealth in parts of southern Europe was primarily a result of their struggles to participate in the Eurasian trade system that thrived under Mongol rule in the thirteenth and fourteenth centuries.

Pirenne's emphasis upon trade meant that European history as usually narrated – the doings of kings and warriors, in which fates were determined in battle, and cultural or other non-material forces such as religion were sometimes critical – was over for most historians, and certainly for all global historians. The proposition that trade could determine the fates of empires and continents was not new, as it was a very important part of Marx's background theories on the contradictions of capitalism. But Pirenne's evidence had all come from studying and thinking about the material lives of common people – what they ate, what they wore, how they earned a living, whether or not they could own land or conduct a lawsuit. Those wishing to criticize his theories had to investigate the same areas of human life. Inevitably the weight of their research shifted toward records of material possessions and the content of trade. Military history was still significant, but tended to become a more material history of weapons, technologies, supplies, and lines of communication. History generally was the story of the long-term changes in the quantity and extent of trade, the use of currency and development of commercial centers, the development of manufacturing and the struggle for efficiency, the ability to back up economic ambitions with diplomatic influence or military force.

Many well-known historians, most of them Europeans, became associated with this movement toward the close study of the material evidence of "everyday life," but the best known today is Fernand Braudel. Like Pirenne, Braudel's historical project was not the study of objects for their meaning or intrinsic importance, but in the context of evidence supporting a much bigger theory of how changes occur on a universal scale. Building on the rich scholarship of the medieval European city-states (to which Pirenne had made a significant contribution), Braudel described a European system in which city-states had stood at the center of semi-independent economic systems, linked among each other by overland and sea routes of longer-distance trade. The dynamics of this meta-system had eventually assimilated the productive agricultural sectors between the systems, producing one large European system of the early modern period that proceeded to incorporate some other parts of the world into a hierarchical network that resembled the way Europe had been both divided and integrated in the medieval period. In its fundamental character, the economy emerging out of the late medieval European system and becoming the model for the early modern world system was capitalist, meaning that – as Marx had predicted – investment itself had become an instrument of production, using ownership and interest rates to leverage natural resources in order to alleviate pressures caused by elites' constant search for higher profits and greater dominance.

While Braudel was still developing his ideas, his student Immanuel Wallerstein provided some of the missing links necessary to describe a much larger system, with separate parts, mutual interaction, and predictable results. For Braudel, the global aspects of his concept had come into play primarily after the consolidation of Europe into a coherent capitalist system and its push to establish a profitable province of markets and resources for itself on other continents, primarily in the seventeenth and eighteenth centuries. For Wallerstein, the process had begun much earlier, and was to be explained not only by the long-term transformations of relationships between labor, wages, productivity, profits, and ownership but also by shorter-term cycles (which Marx had also acknowledged) of expansion and stagnation in the markets (including labor markets). At various points in the development of his model Wallerstein drew upon the concepts of Nikolai Kondratieff (or Kondratiev), a Soviet economist who in the 1920s described and analyzed cycles in European and American economies. Kondratiev refined Marx's basic description of the interactions of supply and demand cycles with the drive for increased profits, predicting that economies of a capitalist nature would experience expansion and stagnation/contraction cycles of roughly forty to sixty years' duration. These "Kondratieff Cycles" (or "Kondratieff Waves") were later refined by Ernest Mandel to illuminate and predict the elements of virtually all social, economic, and even cultural phenomena, as well as episodic disorders such as war and revolution. Joseph Schumpeter has used the similar idea of cyclic price and market fortunes to explain "business cycles" and the way they relate to imperialism and other forms of international competition. In general these ideas came to underlie the school of "political economy" of the very late twentieth century.

What Wallerstein was interested in was how early these cycles could be identified in Europe, and what they would reveal of the functioning of a capitalist system there. He found what he considered clear evidence of capitalist cycling in the thirteenth century. His understanding of the response of the system to periodic crises underlay his theory of the creation and functioning of a "capitalist world system." In 1974, Wallerstein published the first part of his master work, *The Modern World-System* (the second half was published in 1980, the third in 1989, and more volumes are expected). In these books, Wallerstein attempted to explain how Europe's transition out of "feudalism" had created a "world-system" in which Europe constituted a "core" and effectively caused other regions of the world either to take up economic roles at the "periphery" (or "semi-periphery") of this system, or to stay outside the system altogether. In Wallerstein's explanation, the period between about 1450 and about 1650 set the process in motion by which Europe (and by extension North America) came to dominate the rest of the world in the modern period.

Wallerstein's idea was complex and had many interlocking themes, and only its main features can be discussed here. Europe at the end of the "feudal" period was facing several challenges that threatened to strangle its economic expansion. The most fundamental mechanism at work here will be familiar from Marx's idea of decreasing marginal profitability: as it entered the sixteenth century, Europe's agricultural sector produced less wealth per acre than previously. Normal cycling of the economy combined with special pressures from a bloated aristocratic population and changes in the earth's climate produced a "mini ice age." The result was an unprecedented crisis, to which Europe's cities, landowners, and political leaders had to respond. Europe avoided a crash of its economic and social systems at this time, Wallerstein argued, by developing centralized political systems to stabilize the underlying economic systems that Braudel had recognized.

By the mid-seventeenth century the political façades of these market systems became states whose sovereignty was protected by the Westphalian treaties of 1648. Entering the early modern period, European rulers could use new laws, technologies, and economic innovations to undermine the normal control that landowners and aristocrats had exercised over land use in the "feudal" era. Previously, barons would have used their local power and discretion to squeeze more work and more rent out of their peasants, further localizing the trade networks and strangling the flow of money to the king. Now, however, rulers were able to interfere in that cycle, imposing more centralized rule, more standardized practices relating to money and credit, more laws shielding farmers from exploitation by local landholders, and a proportionate weakening of the aristocracies. So-called "absolute monarchies" as they emerged in early-modern Europe were, in Wallerstein's view, vehicles for modernization (though not in themselves "modern"). To reinforce the royal powers, new weaponry such as guns, mortars, and cannon were deployed. The monarchies sponsored the writing of histories and educational programs that created greater cultural uniformity in their own realms and a sharper sense of nationality. The use of more standard ways of writing and speaking within these realms made communications and trade more efficient, while encouraging a rise in general literacy. New laws not only weakened the old economic powers of the landholders, aristocrats, and, in some cases, the Roman Catholic Church, but protected new economic ventures in manufacturing and transport.

The innovations of this period, Wallerstein argued, corresponded with and were mutually reinforced by the maturation of capitalism. Monarchies chartered and often participated in new joint-stock companies, which attracted private wealth to new projects to establish long-distance trade. These companies employed most of the famous "explorers" of the fifteenth and sixteenth centuries to discover the most efficient routes to acquire the raw materials for manufacturing, or the resources – including timber, coal and slaves – to fuel the new industries. The economic expansion led to claims to dominate distant lands and peoples, bringing in more revenue and resources to build armies and economies. In this way, as Wallerstein saw it, Europe accumulated a vastly greater base of capital for further investment, embarking upon a long arc of development in which old wealth created new wealth, and old power generated new power, leading to its peculiar domination of the world in the nineteenth century and the twentieth-century dominance by a Euro-American "West."

In the incorporation of distant regions into this system, Wallerstein saw Europe using the same patterns it had used internally in much earlier times in response to the cyclic stresses of capitalism. Some regions came to function mostly as providers of resources, whether human (serfs or slaves), timber, minerals, or basic crops. Others were market centers, or artisanal and industrial centers. Concentrations of wealth, power, consumption, and industrialization with centralized political power marked the "core" regions, which in the early modern period were mostly England, France, and the Netherlands. Less unified areas with largely raw materials for sale but pockets of industry were part of a "semi-periphery"; Prussia (since Germany was not unified until 1870), Spain (which had once had great centers of wealth and market development but was declining to a politically subordinate position after the 1500s), and British North America were part of this complex zone. Disunified, powerless, and less commercialized regions supplying raw and less finished goods were "peripheries," a category into which Wallerstein put Eastern Europe, Central America and Latin America. Finally, there were large regions that, before 1700, were not part of the world system: Russia, most of Asia, and most of the interior of Africa. In Wallerstein's view, these external areas were neither capitalistic nor commercial, but could become part of the system once their cities became international market centers or their goods became part of the wealth-generating engine of the world system. That happened in the eighteenth century, largely through integration of the Indian Ocean trade system with that of Europe and the development of European imperialism.

Wallerstein built upon the general line of argument, dating to Marx and Engels at the latest, that the rise of Europe to its peculiar power in the nineteenth century had nothing to do with superiority of European culture, and everything to do with the internal dynamics of the developing and periodically decaying capitalist system. It sees feudalism as the necessary antecedent to capitalism, and argues that capitalism could only take full form after the total disappearance of feudalism around 1450. In this theory, the ability of Europe to resolve its recurring crises of profitability depended upon the expanding involvement of new areas of the world, some of which functioned as suppliers of resources and some of which would eventually be important as markets. Independent states had emerged in Europe in parallel with the centrality and influence of their economic centers, and on becoming empire they echoed and magnified the core – periphery patterns from which their own economic strength was born. From their political centers, they manipulated the cross-regional organizations (including but not limited to the great charter companies that colonized North America and managed the Indian Ocean and East Asia trade), allowing royally connected merchants to maximize profits while dampening potentially destabilizing competition. It was a "world" system in the most specific meaning of the word: not universal or global, but limited and defined by the coherence of its internal dynamics and the shared perception of its inhabitants of being inside a continuous and largely predictable system.

As in the case of Pirenne and Bolin, historians were quick to measure Wallerstein's grand theory against the details of European history. Some simply rejected Wallerstein's Marxist and materialist premises, preferring interpretations drawn from Weber and others who considered that culture needed to be a large factor in the explanation of European capitalism and industrialization. Others were skeptical of Wallerstein's dismissal of nationalism and his insistence that the independent states of Europe were only products of the fundamental economic and social dynamics of the region. Some thought that Wallerstein's view of the "Westphalian system" as the definitive expression of European capitalist maturity put too much emphasis on one date and one episode, permanently equating state sovereignty and capitalism in a way that seemed contrary to later history. Still others, sharing Wallerstein's materialist and political economic view of the transition from "feudalism" to "capitalism," were dissatisfied with the rigid classification of some areas as "semi-peripheral" or "peripheral." Robert Brenner, who was associated with studies emphasizing the ways in which market competition, lack of capital resources, and technological innovation were connected, argued that Wallerstein's treatment of the processes by which economic competition at many levels led to the consolidation of European states and their push toward global empires was not sufficiently detailed or supported by historical evidence.

Wallerstein himself has been a critic of what he and many others call "Eurocentrism," by which he means several different things. One is the preference of some scholars for theories that use a hypothesized exceptional or even unique quality of European culture to explain capitalism, industrialization, and imperialism. In Wallerstein's view, the material conditions producing these phenomena in Europe would have produced them anywhere else in the world. But by Eurocentrism, Wallerstein also means to criticize a philosophy of history that regards the production of capitalist wealth and industrial power as the benchmarks of noteworthy or meaningful historical achievement. Wallerstein particularly addressed these criticisms to his critics who conceded that while the basics of his theory were persuasive (as they had been persuasive when first proposed by Marx), the use of Europe as the central line of historical development, with other regions appended to it as "semi-peripheries" or "peripheries," obscured or even denied the degree to which other parts of the world besides Europe had been "feudal" or "capitalist," perhaps even reaching these stages before Europe. In Wallerstein's view, scholars focusing on proving that other areas of the world were "equal" or "earlier" than Europe in achieving capitalism were missing the point. His theory of a world system, after all, presumed the existence of other world systems, some of which may well have been based on something other than capitalism and imperialism. As early modern capitalism and imperialism had in his view grown organically from Europe's medieval dynamics, so other cores would affect their peripheries in ways characteristic of their own social and economic history. The French anthropologist Philippe Beaujard has taken this idea as the subject of his 2007 study of "The Indian Ocean in Eurasian and African World-Systems before the Sixteenth Century."

Some scholars had explored such questions before Wallerstein's work was available to criticize. In the early twentieth century, the Japanese historian Naito Torajiro – not a Marxist but a historian of culture – had argued that China as early as the Song period (tenth to thirteenth centuries) had been "modern." He was referring to the awareness of national distinctiveness; the social mobility produced both by greater access to education because of the spread of printing technologies and by the imperial examinations for appointment to high office; and the increasing influence of merchants in both society and culture. While Naito's ideas in general have continued to influence Chinese studies in Asia, North America, and Europe, he is also the object of much criticism. He argued that China had achieved modernity earlier than any other society, but he also concluded that for complex reasons China had lapsed into a state of "stagnation" in the sixteenth through nineteenth centuries, and that only the challenge and guidance of the imperial powers (including Japan) could reawaken Chinese culture. For this observation Naito was denounced as a sympathizer of or apologist for imperialism. More disturbing to most of his Japanese colleagues was that Naito's "thesis" of China's early modernity was not Marxist or materialist in conception, and that evidence for it could never be objective.

Later historians, perhaps most prominent among them Niida Noboru, were able to revisit Naito's thesis from a Marxist perspective and confirm that China had attained a commercial, capitalist, and "modern" economy and society in the Song period, just as Naito had argued. The theory demanded that China after the fall of the Han empire and before the rise of the Song empire be seen as "feudal" (which most but not all of the Japanese historians tended to call "medieval"), and that the Song period itself demonstrated a growing private sector with basic technologies of book-keeping and credit, more explicit and widespread land rights, social mobility undermining the traditional aristocracy, and capital investment (whether by the state or by private individuals) in industry (in the Song case, primarily coal-mining and steam-operated looms). A group of Japanese historians developed an elaborate body of scholarship, all before the 1970s, describing China in the eleventh century as the world's first modern society and capitalist economy. The fact that China in later centuries had lost its leadership they attributed both to the destructive effects of Mongol and European imperialism, as well as to the internal contradictions of China's early modern capitalism, in which ready availability of cash, labor (due to population growth), and land had stifled reinvestment and technological advancement. The China historian Mark Elvin later adapted and improved upon these elements in his theory of the "high-level equilibrium trap" that explained why a tendency of the economy to exhaust supplies of labor and land to sustain an expanding population had prevented China from continuing its chain of technological innovation and industrial development after the sixteenth century.

Critics of Wallerstein who chose to focus on China as the primary disproof of his theory have produced a great deal of sophisticated scholarship on the varieties of capitalism, the subjectivity of definitions of capitalism, and studies of China's history and society that have avoided assumptions about China that had been deeply embedded in the thought of seminal European scholars such as Hegel, Marx and Weber. Two well-known studies by China scholars, R. Bin Wong's *China Transformed* (1997) and Kenneth Pomeranz's *The Great Divergence* (2000), built on earlier work by scholars of China's economic history to test established ideas of capital and industrial development against China's history of the early modern and modern periods. Wong and Pomeranz both rejected the paradigm of European development as being the normal line of development. In different ways, they described China in the early modern period as working on principles of rational management, legal protection of property, and tendencies toward commercialization that were similar to Europe in the same period. Even levels of material prosperity were similar if certain localities in China and Europe were carefully chosen for comparison. The "divergence" referred to in Pomeranz's title was a relatively late phenomenon, occurring primarily in the nineteenth century, when Europe's imperial powers reached the high point of their military hegemony and their ability to extract resources from other parts of the world.

The two authors had different views of what accounted for the disparity during the nineteenth century. Wong emphasized a certain center of gravity emanating from China's official culture and the continuity of its institutions. Pomeranz recast the well-known interpretations of Europe's extraordinary access to silver and to resources because of its colonization of the Americas in particular. This, Pomeranz argued, was not an organic outgrowth of European patterns of development, as Wallerstein would have had it, but a bit of luck that caused European development to deviate from the more predictable trajectory of capitalism and nation-state definition (which China exemplified in many ways) to its mutated condition of world domination. Scholars steeped in the conventions of Europe-modeled global historiography thrilled at the novelty of these interpretations, and historians

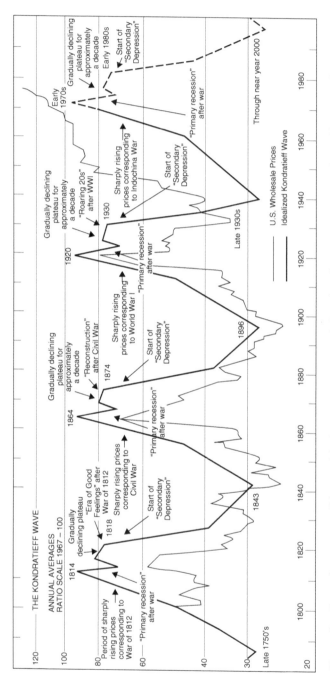

Figure 2　One of many possible graphical representations of the idea that sixty-year Kondratieff waves of economic expansion and contraction can be correlated with events of global significance.

generally were intrigued by the virtuosity with which both authors reinterpreted the available data on Chinese (and to a lesser extent European) development. But in the end Wong and Pomeranz had in their ways restated the issue of Europe's presumed uniqueness in the nineteenth century. Instead of being uniquely normal, as had been the assumption by a central core of global theorists, Europe now looked simply unique. But the contours and significance of its nineteenth-century influence throughout the world appeared to be restated and perhaps emphasized rather than qualified.

A short time after Wong's book was published, the eminent global historian Andre Gunder Frank published his *ReOrient: Global Economy in the Asian Age* (1998). Once a specialist on Latin America, Frank was well known as an economist who had built "dependency theory" upon Wallerstein's foundation; in his early work, Frank and his colleagues had given a systematic description of the limited choices for development and imperatives for exploitation of local resources imposed upon Latin America, Africa, and parts of Asia because of their peripheral relationships to the European "core." In later years, Frank became a critic of many aspects of Wallerstein's theories, especially as they developed in the second and third volumes. In *ReOrient* Frank was the first to integrate many threads of scholarship into a new view of the early modern and modern worlds that was either a direct refutation of Wallerstein or the logical next step on the path Wallerstein had paved.

Recalling the tradition of looking outside Europe for the levers of European wealth that went back through Janet Abu-Lughod to Bolin, Frank argued that the pre-modern sources of European wealth were always to the east, and degrees of European prosperity were related to the efficiency with which Europeans found ways of connecting themselves to the early overland routes to the Middle East and Asia, as well as the later sea routes. During the eleventh to the eighteenth centuries, Frank pointed out, it was the Chinese economy that dominated global development. European middle men – from the Polo brothers of the thirteenth century to the overseers of the great East India companies of the seventeenth century – enriched themselves by becoming agents for European participation in the Chinese economy. The same basic story, with some significant differences, applied to India, Southeast Asia, East Africa, and the Middle East. While giving the Americas their due in the enrichment of early modern Europe, Frank emphasized that it was China's market, and its industrial advancement in ceramics, textiles, and some agricultural products (most famously tea), that created the infrastructure of international trade and the emergence of colonization. Frank saw the period of European dominance in the nineteenth and most of the twentieth centuries as formed by a number of intersecting factors, few of which were exclusive to or original with Europe itself. Most important, he was able to describe modern conditions as not the end of the process of global development, but as an interlude. At the end of this interlude of deviance, he suggested, the more long-term, more fundamental, patterns would effect a correction. China would again be the economy that critically influences the patterns of global trade and wealth.

Frank observed that over time Wallerstein seemed to stray from the strongly materialist origins of his world systems theory and to take culture more and more seriously as a possible explanation for Europe's economic and industrial successes. To Frank, this appeared to be Wallerstein's response to the many dimensions of scholarship that had undermined the foundations of Wallerstein's original theory: the rejection of "feudalism" as a fact by an increasing number of specialists of medieval Europe; the demonstration of economic parity of China and Europe before 1800; the persistent if not well-founded claims of Wallerstein's "Eurocentrism" by scholars in many fields and from many countries. But Frank also suspected that Wallerstein's turn toward cultural explanations, some of them reminiscent of Max Weber, was partly the result of an inability to find any other way to claim that the modern global pre-eminence of Europe and its derivative society in North America was normal, long-lasting, and the organic outcome of millennia of history. To Frank it was obvious that to argue that the situation in which Europe and the United States controlled most of the world's wealth and resources was the normal or cumulative condition of modern history was futile; he regarded any attempts to argue it as contrived and unconvincing on their face. However, the critiques of Frank and others of Wallerstein – and Wallerstein's own response to Wallerstein – were evidence of another kind of change altogether. The historical materialism, the Europe-centered dialectic, and indeed the style of data-oriented economic and social research that had been fundamental to the creation of systems theories dating all the way back to Pirenne in many ways had run its course. World systems theory was, by the end of the twentieth century, regarded as dated and parochial. To the dismay of Andre Gunder Frank, cultural theories were pushing aside the materialist and objectivist systems tradition in global studies.

Suggestions for further reading

Abu-Lughod, Janet, *Before European Hegemony: The World System AD 1250–1350.* New York: Oxford University Press, 1989.
Braudel, Fernand, *Capitalism and Material Life*, trans. Richard Mayne. New York: HarperCollins, 1974.
Chase-Dunn, Christopher and E. N. Anderson, eds, *The Historical Evolution of World-Systems.* New York: Palgrave Macmillan, 2005.
Frank, Andre Gunder, *ReOrient: Global Economy in the Asian Age.* Berkeley CA: University of California Press, 1998.
Pirenne, Henri, *Mohammed and Charlemagne.* New Haven CT: Meridian Books, 1959.
Wallerstein, Immanuel, *World-Systems Analysis: An Introduction.* Raleigh NC: Duke University Press, 2004.

6
What Global History is

In 1997, Wallerstein published a critique of "Eurocentrism" that also attempted to solve what many considered an insoluble riddle. Since social science was an invention of Europeans, based upon the work of European philosophers and historians, how could it become relevant and effective in a global context? The new academic trends of "post-colonial," or "post-modern," studies claimed that the ostensibly objective and absolute intellectual products of Europeans – science, social science, morality, esthetics, and certainly historical narrative – were in fact subjective, self-regarding, ephemeral, and parochial. Wallerstein protested that some disciplines – particularly "science" – were in fact objective, materially based, and universal across cultures. He suggested that science was not the only element of European culture and philosophy that would prove to be universal and enduring. His implication was that dominance by Europe, and subsequently North America, and their ability to define "modernity" in their own image were not haphazard or temporary.

Yet Andre Gunder Frank criticized Wallerstein for abandoning his own materialism and objectivity by championing the cultural achievements of "Western" scientism. It was by rejecting claims of culturalism that Frank was able to account for the temporary shift of wealth generation away from China to Europe as not in itself theoretically problematic or determinative. His general approach of disinterest in European and North American particularism was praised by global historians, many of whom would claim a goal of rooting out the last vestiges of "Eurocentrism" in the writing of global history. But unless these historians adopted the strictly acultural, materialist approach of Frank, it appeared they would come back inevitably to Wallerstein's questions. Global history may be what Douglas Hofstadter popularized as a paradox of self-reference. The telescope cannot regard itself, the computer loop cannot call itself, and global history as an intellectual enterprise is a production of European and American historians who can never make themselves the object of study. This paradox is a launching point for discussing several intersecting and fundamental problems relating to the way we now talk and think about global history.

We might first of all try to determine to what extent global history is actually history. Historians have as their first level of training the acquisition and use of primary documents. This means they must understand the full context in which a historical record is created, and something about the chain of custody from that time to now. They must be skilled in the technologies of document use – languages and writing systems, the ways in which governments and other institutions have preserved and categorized documents, means of determining the authenticity of documents – and they must understand the arts of knowing what is included and what is left out, what is implicit and what is explicit, and what ideology or perspective is controlling the creation of the documents. They must appreciate related sciences or disciplines, such as archeology, anthropology, economics, sociology, or linguistics when such fields may help to contextualize – and to test – the content of the documents. In this respect, historians generating original knowledge must comprehend the local context in minutest detail. Having collected and analyzed all the evidence they can acquire or consult, they must construct an interpretation that tells something about change over time, and produces a story. It is a story merely. Despite the hopes of historians from time to time to adopt the language of scientific objectivity, the physicist makes physics in the laboratory, and the chemist makes chemistry. The historian has no experiments, and no honest use for the "parsimonious" explanations that come from hundreds and

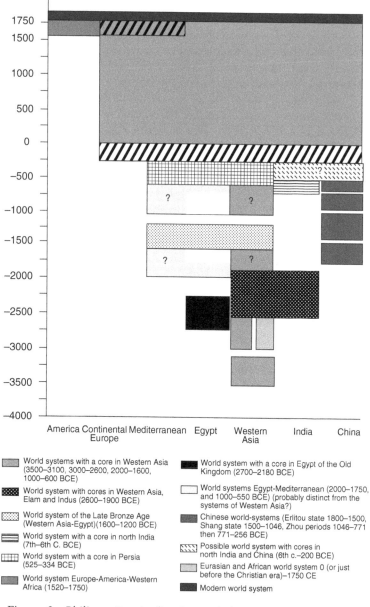

Figure 3 Philippe Beaujard's chart of the interaction of world systems based in seven different centers before 1750. *Source:* Beaujard, "The Indian Ocean in Eurasian and African World-Systems before the Sixteenth Century," p. 418.

thousands of trials and reproductions. The historian makes a story about something he or she can never recreate. It is in this sense that historical study is forensic – what it observes has happened only once, and the historian is forever outside what he hopes to narrate.

In this basic foundation of training and the commitment to generate original knowledge, the historian and the writer of global history have little in common. There is nowhere to go and no method to use for researching global history, since there is no global context for the generation of evidence. Even scholars studying international or comparative subjects must investigate, primarily, the history of specific places, institutions, phenomena, or people. The aspiring writer of global history has little use for the investigatory skills of the historian. It is therefore not surprising that many writers of global history are not historians, but are economists, sociologists, political scientists, scientists, and – as in the case of H. G. Wells – novelists who, like historians, have moved into global history after mastering the basic skills of their own discipline. Historians may of course participate without prejudice, and they have one possible advantage over others in the work: global history closely resembles the historical subdiscipline of historiography, or the study of the writing of history. Like historiographers, global historians must master existing scholarship, which can outweigh in volume by many times the original data available to researchers. And they must deal with very many intersecting areas of scholarship. Also like historiographers, they must be very critical readers of the scholarship, sifting the more reliable from the less reliable, testing suggested hypotheses against others, quite possibly synthesizing their own. In this way, global history becomes a mode of thinking and writing rather than a discipline. In the end, writers must tell a story that aspires to explain global-scale changes over time.

The idea that the past is a story, while found in all cultures, is a perplexing one. Stories have beginnings and ends, main characters and minor characters, themes, morals, and ironies. Few philosophers or historians would regard any of these as actual characteristics of the "past," which is as elusive to define as it is to detect. History is not the past, it is the story we tell to represent the past. Historians hope to tell the story that best fits the totality of the evidence that they can consult, rather than something they have created solely from their wishes or fears. They sometimes agree on the meaning of the evidence, more often they disagree. In all cases, they must use the basic skills of story-building in order to isolate times, places, or topics for study and discussion. They must project beginnings and endings onto the continuous and smooth surface of the "past." It is not unlike trying to build castles on the ocean. Few or no historians actually believe that they are recreating or reviving the past in telling a story. They are representing the past as a narrative arc, for purposes of understanding, and very often for purposes of teaching. The engagement of the imagination, of carefully constructed language to inject the author's interpretation into the representation of past people and events, are all regarded as legitimate if not mistaken as "real." Historians have no ability to capture the past, but hope to capture some fragment of its meaning.

While we can easily distinguish when historians are working in a global mode, it is also important to distinguish between the major and conflicting tasks undertaken by global historians. Up to now in this book we have tended to use the term "global" history to describe all history attempting to address a wide, sweeping, or universal prospect. But this does some injustice to the ways in which global history has developed to the present time, and without further specificity would certainly hamper a discussion of where global history will go from here. Wells, in his *Outline of History*, did not use the word "world" for his history, but tended to say "universal." His word was exact: the story he told proposed some principles of change, particularly revolutionary change, that he regarded as universal not only throughout human history but also through natural history long before humans appeared. We saw that Wallerstein's use of "world" in his story was also exact, and did not mean anything like Wells's "universal." In its derivation "world" means something far more delimited than universe: an age, an era, a milieu, a class, even a totally subjective field in which reality is bent around the perceptions of a single individual. The "world-system" described by Wallerstein was explicitly not global and not universal. It was limited to Europe and those regions of the world that became subordinate to its economy and its military power in a specific span of centuries.

Scholars of global-level history have struggled to follow the outlines of "world" and "global" history as separate genres. Outstanding among this group has been Bruce Mazlish, who as early as 1993 associated inclusive but perhaps haphazard historical compendia as "world" histories, while those focusing on large but coherent patterns appeared to him to be "global." Since then, Mazlish and others have worked to distinguish between works informed by the teleological (or, seeing the past in terms of its known future) problem of early modern and modern European dominance and those focusing on global patterns that may be unrelated to teleologically derived concepts such as "modernity," "development," and "dependence." Out of these efforts have come prescriptions for "new" global histories, much derived from studies of geography and meteorology, paleobotany, physical anthropology, population genetics, neurology (particularly as it relates to language and esthetics), epidemiology, artificial intelligence and computer science, and other materially oriented disciplines that ostensibly transcend (or merely bypass) issues of culture. "Great," "macro," "global," "universal" all remain common terms used by historians yearning to achieve the truly impartial, objective, universal narrative that will transcend narrative teleologies. So far this has not been achieved, probably because history as we know it is written in language, usually prose (as contrasted to pictures, equations, dances, or melody lines), which is linear and subject to perceptions of writer and reader.

Not only are we far from creating a narrative that transcends cultures, few of us have developed global, universal, or "macro" narratives free of the defining, confining, and somehow legitimating reference to the European, capitalist world system that Wallerstein described. The towering outline of Europe's early modern and modern story has been impossible to ignore. First, it had a certain quasi-universalizing function in a field of study without genuine universalization. Everybody everywhere could be characterized in relation to Europe – as an agent or a victim of European domination – and those who had never seen a European (before they saw one) were "undiscovered." Second, the phenomenon of

European domination in the eighteenth and nineteenth centuries was nearly universal. It bent human history in a way that previous empires had not. Whether it was a systematic outgrowth of Europe's earlier history, or it was an anomalous or fortuitous event resulting from accidental discoveries was hardly a very profound matter. The magnitude of the effect was the central fact of human experience in the past three centuries.

Wallerstein's notion of world-system narratives would appear to suggest that any economic center making demands on and limiting the options of subordinated regions, without itself being subordinate to a greater center, would constitute the proper focus of a world-system narrative. Ancient Greece, Iran, Egypt, Zimbabwe, Maya, Aztecs, Incas, Iroquois, Byzantium, Delhi, Songhai, and perhaps an unlimited list of other independent but economically determinative regional centers would be candidates for such treatment, and all would be valuable. But what Wallerstein, Frank, and their critics could neither explain nor rejoice in was the fact that it was, in the end, the European world system that had become the trunk of historical narrative. The nineteenth century, in particular, had become the fulcrum around which a fairly stable set of concepts had revolved. "Modernity" was the condition of being like Europe during and after its industrialization. "Development" and "dependency" marked degrees of economic diversity and discretion associated with distance from the European condition. "Subalternism" was the creation of history from "below," meaning below the domination of European colonialists.

As Frank predicted, we may be closer to a world narrative of China than of other regions. The emergence from the periphery of aggressive military powers (Turks, Mongols, and Manchus), bent upon controlling the unprecedented wealth of the Chinese heartland, is a well-known narrative in Chinese history, used by Owen Lattimore, Franz Michael, Thomas Barfield, and others to explain the long history of "foreign" conquests and occupation of China. The same narrative, with an economic and trade theme, could explain the development of Europe from a peripheral and opportunistic participant in China's world system to a temporary occupier of its economic heart. Frank was close to a story modeled on this, but was

drawing his basic plot from a kind of inversion of Wallerstein, instead of the established histories of China's own cores
and peripheries. In the same way that the Ming empire
emerged centralized and dominant from the period of Mongol
occupation, twenty-first-century China has emerged centralized and dominant from a century and half of European and
Japanese imperialism and interference. This appears to be a
possible goal of a much-discussed but apparently idealized
notion of a "China-centered history" (this means an English-
language history written by foreigners – Chinese, of course,
have always written China-centered history), one that would
free our understanding of the Chinese past from the encompassing framework of European comparisons and the
irrepressible imputations of agency to Europeans and their
cultures in East Asia.

One of the paradoxes of the search for global history is
that the shifts such as that toward a theoretical "Chinese
world-system theory" do not merely de-center Europe as an
orienting point in global narrative, but inevitably reintroduce
culture, often as a monolithic and autonomous actor. The
distinct institutions hypothesized to be the source of a world
system's organization and expansion may be given a new
nominalization, and thus – intentionally or unintentionally –
agency, agenda, and arc. In the case of the modern dominance
produced by the Wallersteinian "world-system," this was
"the West." It had been the gravity of the European impact
on the rest of the world that had inspired the foundation
works of modern global history, which its practitioners –
particularly after the spread of the influence of Wallerstein's
world-system interpretation – called "world history."
Wells had produced *Outline of History* at the height of the
scientific and racialist enthusiasms at the turn of the twentieth
century, and optimistically proposed indefatigable human
evolution toward a future of perfect freedom and enlighten-
ment. In contrast, the troubled German historian Oswald
Spengler wrote *Decline of the West* during the despair of
World War I. The book influenced many disciplines, and not
least history, for its transcendence of the national perspective
and its vision of the coherent interrelation of culture, political
structure, and economic behavior across Europe. It lacked
the specific argumentation and documentary evidence that

historians were looking for, but over time the notion of "the West" as meaning the shared institutions and traditions of Europe was taken as persuasive. When first writing the book during the war, Spengler was consumed by the idea that the West, like other great civilizations, had a saga of rise, dominance, and fall, and that Europe was nearing the end of its story. After the war and Germany's defeat, the book seemed to take on a more uplifting message, which was that German misfortunes were only symptomatic of the degeneration of Europe generally, and would eventually be shared by all Europeans. Later, Spengler's ideas veered into deeper mysticism, paranoid racism, and an enigmatic attitude toward fascism.

Though Spengler's vagueness and his flights through unattractive or outright chilling ideological fancies are usually cited by world historians as reasons to repudiate his work, the underlying schema of "the West" as having a distinct and significant historical trajectory remains fundamental to the writing of world history (the accomplished genre, as distinguished from inchoate global history). A similar position is assumed by many world historians toward the work of the British historian Arnold Toynbee. His twelve volumes of *A Study of History*, which was completed (or ceased being written) in 1961, affirmed the West as a historical character. It wove together several major themes and traditions of British historical writing, particularly Edward Gibbon's panoramic view of the *Fall of the Roman Empire*, with its suggestion that this was the fate of all great civilizations, and Wells's idea of the peripheral origins of innovation and iconoclasm. While perpetuating some of Spengler's mystical philosophy of Western identity, Toynbee was uninterested in Spengler's life-cycle determinism, instead insisting that challenges produced creative responses (at least in the case of genuine civilizations such as the West) that would regenerate cultures afflicted by disastrous wars and depressions.

It is no coincidence that William H. McNeill's best-known and most synthetic work was titled *The Rise of the West* (1963). McNeill's primary criticism of Spengler and Toynbee was that they had equated "West" with "Civilization." Their epics of the rise, sufferings, and triumphs of the West was presented by them as the struggle of civilization over barbarism. But McNeill saw the West as emerging from close competition with other civilizations, particularly China and the Islamic world. The competition was resolved by the end of the early modern period – indeed this resolution in favor or Europe seemed to actually define the onset of the early modern period. Thereafter, Western dominance was consolidated by its control of overseas trade and the colonization of the Americas and Africa, then completed in the nineteenth century with the rise of the United States as an indispensable component of the West and of Western dominance. By the twentieth century, the qualities of Western culture that, in McNeill's view, accounted for its continuing pre-eminence were firmly in place: industrialization, democracy, competitive and mostly capitalist economies, high literacy, and rule of law.

McNeill did not pretend that once the West was dominant its power proved to be a benefit to the vast expanses of the world coming under its sway as colonies, client states, or frontiers. He suggested that the worst predations of the European empires had been moderated by rising American power, which after World War II tended to hasten the end of colonialism. In the now classic narrative strategy of the world history genre (one which Mazlish considers its defining characteristic), McNeill was able to include virtually all the peoples of the earth by relating them to expansion of the European powers and later to the consolidation of American power. The book also makes graceful use of European history as a chronological yardstick, with a sort of "meanwhile back at the ranch" narrative strategy, cutting to "foreign" regions and nations in the Western-derived time frames to catch up on how they were occupying themselves while waiting for the next advance to occur in European wealth and power.

The civilization of the West was not only a concept in the narratives of Spengler, Toynbee, and McNeill, but a philosophy of history in itself: that time and change shape themselves around the destinies of civilizations in general, and Western civilization in particular. For a small number of world historians, it appeared for a time that Western history was actually an absolute: When it fulfilled the maximum potential of its institutional and cultural development, history would end. A formulation of this idea was written by American political scientist Francis Fukuyama, published as the essay, "The End of History?" in 1989 and then as part of the book *The End of History and the Last Man* in 1992. At the time of the writing and publication of the article the Berlin Wall had been torn down, the Soviet Union appeared headed for political disintegration (which happened in 1991), and Eastern Europe was sliding quickly into the economic orbit of Western Europe and the United States. Fukuyama considered these events to signal the transition to the final stage of human history.

The idea that history would end was a widespread one in the foundation works of historical philosophy. Hegel and Marx had both thought that the dialectics of historical change would ultimately conclude. Hegel (whom Fukuyama claimed as his inspiration) had suggested that the end of history would be achieved when the ideal truths of freedom that motivated historical change had been fully realized in human societies. Marx concluded that history would end when class divisions, which were the primary source of contradiction, were eradicated; Chinese communist leader Mao Zedong claimed a break with Marxist theory when he asserted that history can never end, revolution must be eternal along with the need for revolutionary geniuses. Both Hegel and Marx thought that the general course of history was not meandering or accidental, but always tended in the direction of the criteria that would ultimately mark its end. Fukuyama agreed, but argued that the ultimate condition of human society was capitalist and liberal democratic. Once capitalism and liberal democracy had been achieved, ideological differences between human societies would evaporate and history (meaning political evolution) would end.

That time had come, Fukuyama thought, as of about 1991. Thereafter all that would be left to change would be for a few motivated and talented people to oversee the eradication of the last insignificant pockets of undemocratic and uncapitalist backwardness. Fukuyama's argument – or "thesis" as it was called at the time – became instantly a center of attention in the media and in some quarters of the academic world. Only at length did some grasp what Fukuyama had been very clear in stating: The end of history was not going to be a very interesting or even fulfilling period to live through. As it happened, no one needed to worry. The signs were many, and noted by many even when Fukuyama was writing his book, that democracy and capitalism were both being threatened by authoritarian and corporatist developments in the very societies where Fukuyama thought the candle of political transformation had already been snuffed out. In the unlikely case that complete and total liberal democracy and capitalism are actually the conditions that will end history, the world in general – and the self-identified "West" in particular – may still have some dialectical changes to muddle through. For global historians, Fukuyama's book was an example of the intellectual confusions of not only seeing world time as organized by the West but of taking Western experience as the absolute measure of history itself.

Before and after Fukuyama, historians have continued to demonstrate that the ability to narrate arcs of centuries as the story of a civilization was not unique to Europeans, or to Americans seeing themselves as the primary heirs of the West. Chinese historians had two millennia of narrating what they regarded as "civilization," and in the early twentieth century, as the last of the Chinese empires disintegrated, Chinese nationalists adroitly claimed that civilization as a particular national possession, renarrating it as "Chinese civilization." Islamic scholars had a long and sophisticated history – very clearly stretching back to Ibn Khaldun at the latest – of considering their communities, their empires and the extension of Islamic belief as the fundamental theme of all history. English-speaking scholars have also been able to use these alternative civilization narratives to reorganize their understanding of similar historical trends. Perhaps the most dramatic achievement was Marshall Hodgson's three volumes of *The Venture of Islam*, first published in 1974. Since the early 1960s Hodgson had advocated what he called a "hemispheric interregional" approach, which had strong echoes of Pirenne and Bolin. *Venture* was a profound response to the civilizational discourse of the West. As a product of the discourse, Hodgson understood its logic very well, which was to build the history of the medieval and early modern periods, in particular, around the constructed "civilization" itself, making the contours of time and the meaning of change relate to the central ideas and events of the civilization of reference and its ultimate triumph as a leading agent of world change. Hodgson was unapologetic that he himself was neither a Muslim nor a native of a predominantly Muslim society (he was in fact an American Quaker). His story had, as the Western story had, a climactic period of technological, military, and economic dominance, during which the Islamic empires of the Timurid, Mughal, Ottoman, and Safavid empires dominated much of Eurasia as Western Europe played the role of aspiring competitor. As Hodgson pointed out, even the great explosion of European power and influence in the nineteenth and twentieth centuries had been insufficient to suppress the creative cultural energies and evolving societies of the Islamic world; he foresaw the resurgence of international Islamic politics and intellectual life that – not unlike the emergence of modern China as an economic and military power – is in fact shaping the present and future world alongside (and often in opposition to) the ongoing influence of the West.

The perceived coherence and persisting dynamism of both the Islamic and the East Asian spheres has been observed by adherents of the idea of the West, few of whom shared Hodgson's admiration for the Islamic world or his confidence that it represented a creative or humane force in history. They were more likely to be influenced by Bernard Lewis, a British scholar of the Middle East based in the United States, who, beginning in the 1980s, amplified the volume of his warnings against Muslim radicalism as a reaction against Western intrusion and an expression of Muslim hostility against modernity. The Harvard political scientist Samuel Huntington, taking his details from Lewis and his sense of urgency from the sudden popularity of Fukuyama's "end of history" theme, published the article "The Clash of Civilizations?" in 1993. Like his opponent Fukuyama, Huntington later cast off the question mark and used the title for a book (*The Clash of Civilizations and the Remaking of World Order*). Huntington agreed with Fukuyama that with the disappearance of the Soviet Union, the great "ideological" struggle between the West and the communist world had concluded. But according to Huntington that did not mean history was over; competition was, if anything, increasing. The competition would have a superficial nationalist tinge, but in fact would be shaping itself around the identification of societies with cultural traditions – in Huntington's term, "civilizations" – that would each struggle for dominance. The arguments of the "modernization" school, who thought that the attitudes, values, and popular cultures of Europe and the United States would be an homogenizing influence in the world, Huntington argued, were wrong. What instead would happen, particularly now that the discipline of the Cold War had lifted, would be that "East Asian" (sometimes also called "Sinic" or "Confucian") civilization and "Islamic" civilization would push back. Islam would compete with the West for control of oil, while East Asia could compete with the West for markets for manufactured goods.

Huntington's idea of civilizations was not limited to a universe of three, and in fact described the dilemma of most countries in the world that unluckily fell short of the "civilization" league (such as Russia) as forever struggling with the tensions of being at the peripheries or the intersections of the civilizational zones. However, overall Huntington's schema struck most historians as cobbled together from geography books. They pointed out that none of the "civilizations" Huntington's considered real were actually real at all. The Islamic world was sundered by divisions between Sunni and Shi'a; among Arabs, Iranians, Turks, Chinese and Southeast Asians; between more secular and less secular societies. Some countries that were largely Islamic, such as Turkey, were also democratic. Some, such as Afghanistan, had no oil at all. The "Sinic" world was even harder to fit into Huntington's model. Throughout East Asia, nationalist sentiments were profound. The Chinese resented the Japanese, the Koreans resented the Japanese, the Japanese, Koreans, and Vietnamese all resented the Chinese. Neither a single written language nor a single spoken language united them. The lingering question of Taiwan was a bomb waiting to go off. Some parts of East Asia were rapidly industrializing and becoming more aggressive in international competition. Other sectors, even in Japan, were far from industrialization and threatened nobody. But for every ten scholars who objected to Huntington's ideas on factual grounds, there was at least one who saw new opportunities to counsel Western governments and companies on how to counter the nefarious threat posed by the large, hungry, and seamless "civilizations" closing in upon them. And of course those who could identify themselves as the leaders of these imposing civilizations were happy to take up the microphone. The government of Singapore, for instance, became particularly active in promoting the idea of "Sinic" or "Confucian" civilization, sponsoring many academic gatherings of Chinese and Western scholars who wished to produce volumes of essays on their formidable civilization.

Some analysts of international relations came back to Huntington's ideas after the 2001 terrorist attacks in the United States seemed to demonstrate his and Bernard Lewis's predictions of the consequences of Muslim "rage." And awareness of Huntington's "Clash of Civilizations" hypothesis is widespread among among journalists and government officials. But most scholars of global history are not convinced by the idea of cultural determinism. The use of civilization themes by McNeill to narrate the past, they argued, was partly a heuristic device – a way of making something suitable for teaching at the introductory level, which afterwards can be qualified, elaborated, or discarded – for organizing information about the past, and not an assertion that civilizations were objective entities whose fates control the human future.

Many seeking alternatives to the new wave of civilization theory turned to the work of Paul M. Kennedy, *The Rise and Fall of the Great Powers* (1987). Kennedy was an accomplished historian of European military affairs. In his book, he tested many ideas that military historians, from Thucydides to von Clausewitz, had used to analyze the general factors behind sustained military might, and particularly empires. Kennedy augmented his study with review of scholarship on the Ottoman, Russian, and Ming empires, and come to a general conclusion that "overextension" was the fatal flaw, defining the point beyond which they put out more resources than they took in. Most empires had a strategic imperative to continue expansion, since, as Robin Winks had proposed some years before, each expansion brings with it new frontiers that are best secured by expanding beyond them. The longevity of any empire, Kennedy suggested, was influenced by the pace of its expansion and the strategic intelligence applied to defense. Work such as Kennedy's continued the development of structural, fundamentally material, and to some extent systems-oriented analyses that contrasted with the civilization school. In most ways these projects were still identifiably in the "world history" genre. Many were comparative and explicitly sought to study the similarities and contrasts – in urbanization, population growth, women's lives, medical theory and practice – between Europe and selected localities in Asia, the Middle East, or Africa.

An important new development, however, was the emergence of "Indian Ocean" and "Atlantic World" studies. In sharp contrast to the civilization narratives, and even to Wallerstein's idea of narrating from a core region, these new themes took the periphery as the core, regarding the avenues of exchange, whether sea lanes, trading ports, or connected inland market towns and plantations, as the central spine of the narrative. In the case of the Indian Ocean, scholars were able to build coherent histories of the development of long-distance trade and cultural relations between South and Southeast Asia, the Middle East, and East Africa, particularly between about 800 and 1600 CE. China and Europe were both peripheral presences, at least until the remarkable voyages of the Chinese eunuch Zheng He through the entire Indian Ocean system in the early 1400s and the large-scale intrusions of European colonialists and mercantilists after 1600. The ability to use the Indian Ocean as a matrix for discrete and concrete studies of technologies, Islamic influences, and economic development has shaped an extremely productive subgenre of world history that will probably only continue to deepen its methodological sophistication and conceptual coherence. Though initiated later than Indian Ocean studies, Atlantic World has also emerged as an exceptionally rich field for the comparative and systems study of the relations between Western Europe, North Africa, West Africa, the Caribbean, and Latin America. The Caribbean in particular has emerged in very sharp focus, as a nexus point of transformative influence in both the economic and the political fortunes of Europe and North America. The movement of peoples, languages, religions, crops, and diseases laid the foundation for a minimum of four centuries of interaction, some of it strongly shaped by the universal involvement of the Atlantic populations in one aspect or another of slave trading. In the same spirit, Mediterranean history has been recentered, giving us new access to our understanding of trade, linguistic, and genetic history in the region.

Related to the creation of Indian Ocean and Atlantic World studies as distinct discursive environments, but also having an internal dynamic of its own, has been the subgenre of "encounter" or "exchange" scholarship. Its best-known practitioner has been the American historian Jerry Bentley, who has not only worked to present the content of transformational encounters but has also proposed that global history can be periodized according to changes in the character and frequency of cross-cultural contacts. This was an attempt to break free of the conventional chronology defined by European experience. Bentley sees the increasing frequency and the changing content of encounters as a variable produced by progressive developments in trade and technology, not determined by states, cultures, or "civilizations." The periods he marks out, however, do not look greatly different from those proposed earlier by Morgan, Marx, or Wallerstein. The "feudal" period is displaced by a post-classical age between about 500 and 1000 CE, and the period from 1000 to 1500 is an age of "nomadic empires." But 1500 is intact as the conventional landmark between overland and overseas trade (something that Indian Ocean world historians, in particular, must see as parochially Eurocentric). The ancient, classical, and modern periods are pretty much where one would expect to find them. Bentley's approach is appealing for a variety of reasons. Since there are documents relating to events such as encounters, the study of these moments comes closest to establishing something actually researchable in global history. It is also eminently effective for teaching, bringing the immediacy of past experience to the reader. But, as other scholars (for example, Patrick Manning) have pointed out, there are also important questions that arise. Are cross-cultural contacts, and the experience of encounter itself, the true stuff of global history?

These questions are pressing because Bentley, Manning, and many of their colleagues have represented a vanguard of scholars working to break away from the "world" history genre and to create a true discipline – with a chronology, an analytical focus, and an explanation – of "global" history. To do this they must bypass the European-derived notions of "feudalism" (thus Bentley paints over the medieval period), "modernity," "the West," "westernization," "industrialization," and so on. They must also have a scheme that is easy to teach. The primary heuristic device emerging so far from this genre has been a sort of pyramidical understanding of the inverse relationship between time and diversity. At the beginning of human history, there is more diversity, at the end of human history, there is little or none. This is because human communities start out small and widely spaced (few or no encounters). They discover agriculture and their populations grow. The "cultural cores" (to invoke a convention used in textbook construction) expand, creating the early empires, from Sumeria to Rome and Han. The expanding cores touch, trade, and conflict with each other (more and more encounters). Contact causes a rise in knowledge of each other and in cultural exchange (as in the period of Charlemagne and Harun al-Rashid), but it is still modest. Under the Mongol-dominated empires of the thirteenth century, the volume and distance of contacts rises sharply, promoting more contact. With the rise of the great European sea-powers after 1480, the whole globe comes into communication; encounters rise ever more steeply in frequency and become more and more a conduit of acculturation. In the modern period, the addition of mass media completes the cultural character of contact, putting the "globalization" into global history.

As a framework for narrating global cultures without obviously privileging one or the other, the pyramid scheme works well, and it has an appealing resonance with the implied chronologies of the contagion historians, particularly Crosby and McNeill. But most historians are aware that it conflicts rather fundamentally with history as it is known. The earliest humans do not in fact appear to have represented the extremes of human diversity. Population historians are still debating when and where there may have been bottlenecks in very early human history, resulting in a very small number of closely allied survivors who only in time expanded again in space and in population. But even when Paleolithic humans were fairly numerous and living everywhere except Antarctica, their cultures were not extremely different from each other. It was agriculture that produced the stunning diversity of classical civilizations. In total it would appear that the actual history of human diversity is more football-like, vase-like, or violin-like than pyramidal. Moreover, it is not clear that decreasing diversity and increasing contact have a straightforward relationship. We now know that ancient peoples had trading networks that covered many thousands of miles, spreading goods and technologies from one end of Eurasia to another, from North to South America and back again. The frequency or the character of contacts – at what point did they commonly involve repeat visits, learning of languages, intermarriage? – even in very early times is difficult to characterize with confidence. If high-frequency, full-spectrum contact is really acculturating, we should find diversity in the modern world decreasing. Forty years ago that was assumed to be the case. Now we see that in fact disparities in privilege, security, and perceptions of power generate new cultural differences both within single societies and across continental and regional divides. New cultures are constantly emerging – ways of speaking, standards of public behavior, esthetic criteria, morals, music, dress, and even assumptions on whether things like science and political structures are real. Patrick Manning, in a critique of Bentley's "encounter" model, suggests something of this when he points out that "culture" and its definition are not more objective propositions than "modernity," or "civilization," or "development" had been. If one cannot define a culture, how does one know when one culture is encountering another? It would appear that, as with all forms of history, global historians must struggle with the problem of working back from an axiomatic "event" to the reconstruction of its elements. It is a hazardous process, and one that – unlike Hegel's and Marx's history – can never come to an end. Global historians aspire to find the keys to the human condition – seeing beyond the distortions of the last few centuries, seeing through the superficial edifices left by empires and hegemonies, to the forces shaping human fortunes over the entire past, and into the future.

Suggestions for further reading

Chaudhuri, K. N., *Asia before Europe: Economy and Civilization in the Indian Ocean from the Rise of Islam to 1750*. Cambridge: Cambridge University Press, 1990.

Fukuyama, Francis, *The End of History and the Last Man*. New York: Free Press, 1992.

Hodgson, Marshall G. S., *The Venture of Islam, Conscience and History in a World Civilization, Volume 3: The Gunpowder Empires and Modern Times* (reprint). Chicago IL: University of Chicago Press, 1977.

Huntington, Samuel P., *The Clash of Civilizations and the Remaking of World Order*. New York: Simon & Schuster, 1996.

Spengler, Oswald, *The Decline of the West* (2 vols), trans. C. F. Atkinson. New York: Alfred A. Knopf, 1922.

Toynbee, Arnold J., *A Study of History* (12 vols). Oxford: Oxford University Press, 1934–61.

Bibliography

Abu-Lughod, Janet, *Before European Hegemony: The World System AD 1250–1350*. New York: Oxford University Press, 1989.

Akyeampong, Emmanuel Kwaku, *Themes in West Africa's History* (Western African Studies). Columbus OH: Ohio University Press, 2006.

Arrighi, Giovanni, *The Long Twentieth Century: Money, Power and the Origins of our Times*. London: Verso, 1987.

Arrighi, Giovanni and Beverly J. Silver, eds, *Chaos and Governance in the Modern World System*. Minneapolis MN: University of Minnesota Press, 1999.

Asakawa, Kan'ichi, *The Documents of Iriki, Illustrative of the Development of Feudal Institutions of Japan*. (Reprint) Westport CT: Greenwood Press, 1974.

Beaujard, Philippe, "The Indian Ocean in Eurasian and African World-Systems before the Sixteenth Century," *Journal of World History*, vol. 16, no. 4 (2005), pp. 411–66.

Benjamin (of Tudela), *The Itinerary of Benjamin of Tudela: Travels in the Middle Ages*, trans. Joseph Simon. Malibu CA: Pangloss Press, 1993.

Bentley, Jerry H., "Hemispheric Integration, 500–1500 CE," *Journal of World History*, vol. 9, no. 2 (1998), pp. 237–54.

Bentley, Jerry H., *Old World Encounters: Cross-Cultural Contacts and Exchanges in Pre-Modern Times*. Oxford & London: Oxford University Press, 1993.

Bentley, Jerry H., "Myths, Wagers, and Some Moral Implications of World History," *Journal of World History*, vol. 16, no. 1 (2005), pp. 51–82.

Benton, Lauren A., "From the World-Systems Perspective to Institutional World History: Culture and Economy in Global Theory," *Journal of World History*, vol. 7, no. 2 (1996), pp. 261–95.

Blaut, James M., ed., *Fourteen Ninety-Two: The Debate on Colonialism, Eurocentrism and History*. Trenton NJ: Africa World Press, 1992.

Blaut, James M., *The Colonizer's Model of the World: Geographical Diffusionism and Eurocentric History*. New York: Guilford Press, 1993.

Bosworth, Andrew, "The Evolution of the World-City System, 3000 BCE to AD 2000," in Robert A. Denemark et al., eds, *World System History: The Social Science of Long-Term Change*. London: Routledge, 2000.

Braudel, Fernand, *Capitalism and Material Life*, trans. Richard Mayne. New York: HarperCollins, 1974.

Braudel, Fernand, *The Perspective of the World: Civilization and Capitalism 15th to 18th Century, Volume 3*, trans. Sian Reynolds. New York: HarperCollins, 1984.

Braudel, Fernand, *Civilization and Capitalism 15th to 18th Century, Volume 2: The Wheels of Commerce*, trans. Sian Reynolds. New York: HarperCollins, 1986.

Braudel, Fernand, *Civilization and Capitalism, 15th to 18th Century, Volume I: The Structures of Everyday Life: The Limits of the Possible*, trans. Sian Reynolds. Berkeley CA: University of California Press, 1992.

Braudel, Fernand, *A History of Civilizations*. New York: Penguin, 1995.

Bulliet, Richard W., *The Camel and the Wheel*. Cambridge MA: Harvard University Press, 1975.

Burke, Edmund III, "Islamic History as World History: Marshall Hodgson, 'The Venture of Islam,'" *International Journal of Middle Eastern Studies*, vol. 10, no. 2 (1979), pp. 241–64.

Carr, E. H., *What is History?* (with a new introduction by Richard J. Evans). Basingstoke: Palgrave, 2001.

Cavalli-Sforza, Luigi Luca and Francesco Cavalli-Sforza, *The Great Human Diasporas: The History of Diversity and Evolution*. New York: Addison-Wesley, 1995.

Cavalli-Sforza, P. Menozzi and A. Piazza, *The History and Geography of Human Genes*. Princeton NJ: Princeton University Press, 1994.

Chase-Dunn, Christopher and E. N. Anderson, eds, *The Historical Evolution of World-Systems*. New York: Palgrave Macmillan, 2005.

Chaudhuri, K. N., *Asia before Europe: Economy and Civilization in the Indian Ocean from the Rise of Islam to 1750*. Cambridge: Cambridge University Press, 1990.

Chew, Sing C., *World Ecological Degradation: Accumulation, Urbanization and Deforestation: 3000 BC–AD 2000*. Walnut Creek CA: AltaMira, 2001.

Christian, David, *A History of Russia, Central Asia and Mongolia, Vol. 2: Inner Eurasia from Prehistory to the Mongol Empire*. Malden MA: Blackwell, 1998.

Cipolla, Carlo, *Guns, Sails and Empires: Technological Innovation and the Early Phases of European Expansion 1400–1700*. New York: Minerva Press, 1965.

Crosby, Alfred W., *The Columbian Exchange: Biological and Cultural Consequences of 1492*. Westport CT: Greenwood Press, 1972.

Crosby, Alfred, *Ecological Imperialism: The Biological Expansion of Europe, 900–1900*. Cambridge: Cambridge University Press, 1986.

Crosby, Alfred W., *America's Forgotten Pandemic: The Influenza of 1918*. Cambridge: Cambridge University Press, 2004.

Cunliffe, Barry, *Facing the Ocean: The Atlantic and its People*. Oxford & New York: Oxford University Press, 2001.

Dale, Stephen F., "Ibn Khaldun: The Last Greek and the First Annaliste Historian," *International Journal of Middle East Studies*, vol. 38 (2006), pp. 431–51.

Dale, Stephen F., *Indian Merchants and Eurasian Trade, 1600–1750*. Cambridge: Cambridge University Press, 2002.

de Boer, Jelle Zeilinga and Donald Theodore Sanders, *Earthquakes in Human History: The Far-Reaching Effects of Seismic Disruptions*. Princeton NJ: Princeton University Press, 2004.

Denemark, Robert A. et al., eds, *World System History: The Social Science of Long-Term Change*. London: Routledge, 2000.

Dewald, Carolyn and John Marincola, eds, *The Cambridge Companion to Herodotus*. Cambridge: Cambridge University Press, 2006.

Diamond, Jared, *Guns, Germs and Steel: The Fates of Human Societies*. New York: W. W. Norton, 1997.

Donner, Fred, *Narratives of Islamic Origins*. Princeton NJ: Darwin Press, 1998.

Drews, Robert, *The Coming of the Greeks: Indo-European Conquests in the Aegean and the Near East*. Princeton NJ: Princeton University Press, 1994.

Drews, Robert, *The End of the Bronze Age*. Princeton NJ: Princeton University Press, 1995.

Dunn, Ross E., *The New World History: A Teacher's Companion*. Boston MA: Bedford/St Martin's, 1999.

Dunn, Ross E., *The Adventures of Ibn Battuta: A Muslim Traveler of the Fourteenth Century*. Berkeley CA: University of California Press, 2004.

Durham, William H., *Coevolution: Genes, Culture and Human Diversity*. Stanford CA: Stanford University Press, 1991.

Ehret, Christopher, *An African Classical Age: Eastern and Southern Africa in World History, 1000 BC to AD 400*. Charlottesville VA: University of Virginia Press, 2001.

Elvin, Mark, *The Pattern of the Chinese Past*. Stanford CA: Stanford University Press, 1973.

Fernández-Armesto, Felipe, *Pathfinders: A Global History of Exploration*. New York: W. W. Norton, 2006.

Finkelstein, David and Alistair McCleery, *An Introduction to Book History*. London: Routledge, 2005.

Foucault, Michel, *The History of Sexuality: An Introduction*. (Reissue) New York: Vintage, 1990.

Frank, Andre Gunder, *ReOrient: Global Economy in the Asian Age*. Berkeley CA: University of California Press, 1998.

Frank, Andre Gunder and Barry K. Gills, *The World System: Five Hundred Years or Five Thousand?* London: Routledge, 1993.

Freese, Barbara, *Coal: A Human History*. New York: Perseus Books Group, 2003.

Fukuyama, Francis, *The End of History and the Last Man*. New York: Free Press, 1992.

Fukuyama, Francis, *Our Posthuman Future: Consequences of the Biotechnology Revolution*. New York: Picador, 2003.

Gibbon, Edward, *The Decline and Fall of the Roman Empire* (6 vols). London: Penguin Classics, 1983.

Goldstone, Jack. A., "Cultural Orthodoxy, Risk and Innovation: The Divergence of East and West in the Early Modern World," *Sociological Theory*, vol. 5, no. 1 (1987), pp. 119–35.

Haas, Jonathan, "On Diffusion, Diffusionism, and Cultural Materialism," *American Anthropologist*, vol. 79, no. 3 (1977), pp. 649–52.

Hall, John, *Powers and Liberties: The Causes and Consequences of the Rise of the West*. New York & London: Oxford University Press, 1986.

Herodotus, *The Histories*, trans. Robin Waterfield. New York: Oxford University Press, 1998.

Hodgson, Marshall G. S., *Rethinking World History*. Cambridge: Cambridge University Press, 1993.

Hodgson, Marshall G. S., *The Venture of Islam, Conscience and History in a World Civilization, Volume 1: The Classical Age* (reprint). Chicago IL: University of Chicago Press, 1977.

Hodgson, Marshall G. S, *The Venture of Islam, Conscience and History in a World Civilization, Volume 2: The Expansion of Islam in the Middle Periods* (reprint). Chicago IL: University of Chicago Press, 1977.

Hodgson, Marshall G. S, *The Venture of Islam, Conscience and History in a World Civilization, Volume 3: The Gunpowder Empires and Modern Times* (reprint). Chicago IL: University of Chicago Press, 1977.

Horden, Peregrine and Nicholas Purcell, *The Corrupting Sea: A Study of Mediterranean History.* Oxford & London: Blackwells Publishers, 2000.

Hourani, Albert, *A History of the Arab Peoples.* Cambridge MA: Harvard University Press, 1991.

Hughes, Sally Smith, *The Virus: A History of a Concept.* New York: Heinemann Educational Books, 1977.

Huntington, Samuel P., *The Clash of Civilizations and the Remaking of World Order.* New York: Simon & Schuster, 1996.

Jones, H. L., *The Geography of Strabo.* New York: Loeb Classical library, 1917–32.

Kennedy, Paul M., *The Rise and Fall of the Great Powers: Economic Change and Military Conflict from 1500 to 2000.* New York: Vintage, 1987.

Kotkin, Joel, *The City: A Global History* (Modern Library Chronicles). New York: Modern Library, 2005.

Kristiansen, Kristian and Michael Rowlands, *Social Transformation in Archaeology: Global and Local Perspectives.* London: Taylor & Francis (Routledge), 1998.

Kuhn, Thomas S., *The Structure of Scientific Revolutions* (3rd edn). University of Chicago IL: University of Chicago Press, 1996.

Kurlansky, Mark, *Salt: A World History.* New York: Penguin, 2003.

Landes, David S., *The Wealth and Poverty of Nations: Why Some are so Rich and Some so Poor.* New York: W. W. Norton, 1998.

Lieberman, Victor, "Transcending East–West Dichotomies: State and Culture Formation in Six Ostensibly Different Areas," *Modern Asian Studies*, vol. 31, no. 1 (1997), pp. 463–546.

Liu, Xinru, *Ancient India and Ancient China: Trade and Religious Exchanges, AD 1–600.* New Delhi: Oxford University Press, 1988.

Manning, Patrick, "The Problems of Interactions in World History," *American Historical Review*, vol. 101, no. 3 (1996), pp. 771–82.

Manning, Patrick, *Navigating World History: Historians Create a Global Past*. New York: Palgrave Macmillan, 2003.

Marks, Robert B., *The Origins of the Modern World: A Global and Ecological Narrative from the Fifteenth to the Twenty-first Century*. Lanham MD: Rowman & Littlefield, 2006.

Marx, Karl, *Capital: An Abridged Edition*, ed. David McLellan. Oxford: Oxford University Press, 1999.

Mazlish, Bruce, *The Riddle of History: The Great Speculators from Vico to Freud*. New York: Harper & Row, 1966.

Mazlish, Bruce, *The New Global History*. London: Routledge, 2006.

Mazlish, Bruce and Ralph Buultjens, eds, *Conceptualizing Global History*. Boulder CO: Westview, 1993.

Mazlish, Bruce and Akira Iriye, *The Global History Reader*. London: Routledge, 2005.

McNeill, John Robert, *Something New Under the Sun: An Environmental History of the Twentieth-Century World*. New York: W. W. Norton, 2001.

McNeill, William H., *The Rise of the West: A History of the Human Community*. Chicago IL: University of Chicago Press, 1963.

McNeill, William H., *Plagues and Peoples*. Garden City NJ: Doubleday/Anchor, 1976.

McNeill, William H., *The Human Condition: An Ecological and Historical View*. Princeton NJ: Princeton University Press, 1980.

McNeill, William H., *Keeping Together in Time: Dance and Drill in Human History*. Cambridge MA: Harvard University Press, 1997.

Melko, Matthew, "The Interaction of Civilizations: An Essay," *Journal of World History*, vol. 9, no. 4 (1969), pp. 559–77.

Mokyr, Joel, *The Lever of Riches: Technological Creativity and Economic Progress*. Oxford: Oxford University Press, 1990.

Montgomery, James E., "Ibn Fadlan and the Rusiyyah," *Journal of Arabic and Islamic Studies*, vol. 3 (2000), pp. 1–25.

Morgan, Lewis Henry, *Ancient Society: Or, Researches in the Lines of Human Progress from Savagery through Barbarism to Civilization*. Boston MA: Adamant Media Corporation, 2004.

Nakamura, Hajime, *Parallel Developments: A Comparative History of Ideas*. New York: Harper & Row, 1975.

Northrup, David, *Africa's Discovery of Europe: 1450–1850*. New York: Oxford University Press, 2002.

Pacey, Arnold, *Technology in World Civilization: A Thousand-Year History*. Cambridge MA: MIT Press, 1990.

Perry, Matt, *Marxism and History*. New York: Palgrave Macmillan, 2002.

Pirenne, Henri, *Medieval Cities: Their Origins and the Revival of Trade*, trans. Frank D. Halsey. Princeton NJ: Princeton University Press, 1952.

Pirenne, Henri, *Mohammed and Charlemagne*. New Haven CT: Meridian Books, 1959.

Pirenne, Jacques, *The Tides of History*. London: Routledge, 2006.

Polanyi, Karl, *The Great Transformation* (reprint). Boston MA: Beacon Press, 2001.

Pomeranz, Kenneth, *The Great Divergence: China, Europe and the Making of the Modern World Economy*. Princeton NJ: Princeton University Press, 2000.

Renfrew, Colin, *Systems Collapse as Social Transformation: Approaches to Social Archeology*. Edinburgh: Edinburgh University Press, 1984.

Renfrew, Colin, *Archaeology and Language*. London: Jonathan Cape, 1987.

Reynolds, Susan, *Fiefs and Vassals: The Medieval Evidence Reinterpreted*. New York: Oxford University Press, 1996.

Robinson, Chase, *Islamic Historiography*. Cambridge: Cambridge University Press, 2003.

Rossabi, Morris, *Voyager from Xanadu: Rabban Sauma and the First Journey from China to the West*. New York: Kodansha International, 1992.

Rowlands, Michael et al., eds, *Centre and Periphery in the Ancient World*. Cambridge: Cambridge University Press, 1987.

Shboul, Ahmad A. M., *Al-Mas'udi and his World*. London: Ithaca Press, 1979.

Sima Qian, *Records of the Grand Historian*, trans. Burton Watson. New York: Columbia University Press, 1993.

Simoni, L. et al., "Reconstruction of Prehistory on the Basis of Genetic Data," *Journal of Human Genetics*, vol. 66, no. 3 (2000), pp. 1177–9.

Skocpol, Theda, "Wallerstein's World Capitalist System: A Theoretical and Historical Critique," *American Journal of Sociology*, vol. 82, no. 5 (1977), pp. 1075–90.

Smyser, H. M., "Ibn Fadlan's Account of the Rus with Some Commentary and Some Allusions to Beowulf," in Jess B. Bessinger, Jr. and Robert P. Creed, eds, *Franciplegius: Medieval and Linguistic Studies in Honor of Francis Peabody Magoun, Jr*. New York: New York University Press, 1965, pp. 92–119.

Spengler, Oswald, *The Decline of the West* (2 vols), trans. C. F. Atkinson. New York: Alfred A. Knopf, 1922.

Staller, John, Robert Tykot and Bruce Benz, eds, *Histories of Maize: Multidisciplinary Approaches to the Prehistory, Linguistics, Bio-*

geography, Domestication and Evolution of Maize. San Diego CA: Academic Press, 2006.

Stockdale, Melissa Kirschke, *Paul Miliukov and the Quest for a Liberal Russia.* Ithaca NY: Cornell University Press, 1996.

Tinbergen, Jan, *Lessons from the Past.* Amsterdam: Elsevier, 1963.

Toynbee, Arnold J., *A Study of History* (12 vols). Oxford: Oxford University Press, 1934–61.

Trask, R. L., *Historical Linguistics.* London: Arnold, 1996.

Vainker, Shelagh, *Chinese Silk: A Cultural History.* New Brunswick NJ: Rutgers University Press, 2004.

Wallerstein, Immanuel, *The Modern World System: Capitalist Agriculture and the Origins of the European World Economy in the Sixteenth Century.* San Diego CA: Academic Press, 1974.

Wallerstein, Immanuel, *The Modern World-System, II: Mercantilism and Consolidation of the European World-Economy, 1600–1750.* San Diego CA: Academic Press, 1980.

Wallerstein, Immanuel, *The Modern World-System III: The Second Era of Great Expansion of the Capitalist World-Economy, 1730s–1840s.* San Diego CA: Academic Press, 1989.

Wallerstein, Immanuel, "The Inventions of TimeSpace Realities: Towards an Understanding of our Historical Systems," in *Unthinking Social Science.* Cambridge: Polity Press, 1991, pp. 135–48.

Wallerstein, Immanuel, "Eurocentrism and its Avatars: The Dilemmas of Social Science," *New Left Review,* vol. 226 (Nov–Dec 1997), pp. 93–107.

Wallerstein, Immanuel, *World-Systems Analysis: An Introduction.* Raleigh NC: Duke University Press, 2004.

Watson, Andrew M., *Agricultural Innovation in the Early Islamic World: The Diffusion of Crops and Farming Techniques, 700–1100.* Cambridge: Cambridge University Press, 1983.

Watts, Sheldon, *Epidemics and History: Disease, Power and Imperialism.* New Haven CT: Yale University Press, 1997.

Weber, Max, *Economy and Society: An Outline of Interpretive Sociology,* trans. G. Roth and C. Wittich. New York: Bedminster Press, 1968.

Wells, Herbert George, *The Outline of History: Being a Plain History of Life and Mankind.* New York: The Macmillan Company, 1920.

Whitfield, Susan, *Life Along the Silk Road.* Berkeley CA: University of California Press, 2000.

Wilkinson, David, "Central Civilization," in Stephen K. Sanderson, ed. *Civilization and World Systems.* Walnut Creek CA: AltaMira Press, 1995, pp. 46–4.

Wong, R. Bin, *China Transformed: Historical Change and the Limits of European Experience*. Ithaca NY: Cornell University Press, 1997.

Zinsser, Hans, *Rats, Lice and History: being a study in biography which, after twelve preliminary chapters indispensable for the preparation of the lay reader, deals with the life history of typhus fever*. New York: Bantam Books, 1967.

Index